# THE DISCOVERERS

## THE LIVING PAST

The early discoverers had to overcome real and imagined dangers and endure weariness, starvation and disease in their search for trade routes and new lands. In the early days, sailors crossed unknown seas with simple navigational instruments in ships that were surprisingly cramped and ill-equipped for making long sea journeys. This beautifully illustrated book tells the exciting story of how the map of our modern world was slowly, and painfully, built up over the centuries by men who were often ruthless adventurers but also brave and far-sighted discoverers.

ARCO PUBLISHING, INC.
New York

Published by Arco Publishing, Inc.
219 Park Avenue South, New York, N.Y. 10003

Copyright © 1979, 1981 by Marshall Cavendish Ltd.

All rights reserved

Printed and bound in Hong Kong

This book may not be sold outside of the United States of America, its territories and Canada.

Library of Congress Cataloging in Publication Data

Main entry under title:

The Discoverers.

(The Living past)
Includes index.
SUMMARY: Discusses early explorers and the results of their exploration on the cultures and economies of both old and new worlds.
1. Explorers—Biography—Juvenile literature.
[1. Explorers]
G200.D52  910'.92'2  [B]  [920]  79-11548
ISBN 0-668-04784-4

# Acknowledgements

**Author:**
Neil Grant
**Adviser:**
Ann Savours
**Editors:**
Jo Jones
Trisha Pike
**Art Editor:**
John Curnoe
**Picture Researchers:**
Anne-Marie Ehrlich
Julia Calloway

**Illustrations:**
John Berry/John Martin and Artists
12/13, 35; Harry Bishop/Linda Rogers
Associates 40; Gino D'Achille 54;
Peter Dennis/Linda Rogers Associates
10-11; Eugene Fleury Maps 16, 20,
24-25, 28, 31, 32, 34, 36, 38, 40, 44, 46,
48; Oliver Frey/Temple Art 47; John
Green/John Martin & Artists 36; John
Hampson/John Martin & Artists 18-19;
Richard Hook 8, 27, 30-31; John Hunt/
John Martin & Artists cover, 16; Ivan
Lapper/Linden Artists 22-23; David
Nockels 32-33; Nigel Osborne 14-15.

**Pictures:**
Bibliothèque Nationale 7(B), 9(R), 16,
22-3, 42-3; Bodleian Library 6-7, 7(T),
18(R), 39, 42, 54-5, 57(T); Reproduced
by permission of the British Library 6,
17(TR), 17(B), 26-7, 47, 55; Courtesy of
the British Museum 43(T), (Natural
History) 45(TR), 48(R); City of Bristol
Art Gallery 32(B); Bruce Coleman

34–5(T); Werner Forman Archive
28(B); Giraudon 21, end papers;
Michael Holford 18(L), 19, 31, 48, 50;
Huntingdon Library, San Marino,
California 32-3; Alan Hutchison
Library 17 (TL); F. Lane 38 (B); Mansell
Collection 34–5(B), 52(L); Mariners'
Museum, Virginia 24-5, 52(R); Mas
28(T), 29, 56(R); Courtesy of Lord
Middleton 38(T); Musée des Beaux
Arts, Quimper 25; National Library of
Australia 57(B); National Maritime
Museum 4, 8, 9 (L), 11, 13, 41, 44–5 and
46 (on loan from Ministry of Defence,
Navy), 49 (B), 53 (Greenwich Hospital
Collection); MauroPucciarelli 43 (C);
Queen Victoria Museum, Hobart
45(TL); Radio Times Hulton Picture
Library 26(B); Réunion des Musées
Nationaux 23; Royal Geographical
Society 51; Salmer 30; Scala 27; Charles
Swithinbank 37(T); Courtesy of the
Trustees of the Tate Gallery 37(B);
Eileen Tweedy 49(T); University of
Witwatersrand, Johannesburg 20–21.

# Contents

# The Eve of Adventure

Six hundred years ago all travel was difficult and dangerous. Most people in Europe lived in the same place all their lives. A journey to the next town was something to talk about, and only churchmen, merchants, diplomats and soldiers traveled to foreign countries. Travel for pleasure belonged to the future; no one went anywhere unless he had to.

A journey by land, on foot or on horseback, along deserted tracks that disappeared in muddy marshes or tangled forests, was hard enough. A sea voyage was worse. Ships hugged the coastline nervously, fearful of storms and shipwreck. People who had to cross the English Channel or the calmer Mediterranean prayed earnestly for their safety and gave thanks to God when they reached the other side.

Some people had made long journeys in the past. For instance, in the tenth century, the Vikings had crossed the North Atlantic, settling in Greenland and visiting North America. Later, the Crusaders had gone to fight in the Holy Land, and Italian merchants such as Marco Polo had visited China. But Marco Polo's story of his adventures in the Far East was treated as a fairy tale, and the voyages of the Vikings had been forgotten. The Atlantic Ocean, the 'Green Sea of Darkness' as the Arabs called it, lay mysterious and unconquered. No one knew where it ended, or if it ended at all. It was a greater mystery to our ancestors than the stars and the planets in outer space are to us.

The little that was known of lands far distant from Europe was a mixture of fact and fancy. Knowledge was based on travelers' tales (some true, some false), on ancient legends, on fears of the unknown, and on hopes of finding a better place. According to the Bible, the Garden of Eden was to be found somewhere 'in the East'. Some map-makers, therefore, hopefully marked it on their maps. India was known to exist somewhere east of Europe, but the 'India' that people imagined was more like a

Above: The *mappa-mundi* ('map of the world') in the Middle Ages, based on religious teaching, looked nothing like the real world. The Bible said that Jerusalem was the center of the world, and the map-makers took that statement literally. The earth was shown as a flat disc, made up of the three known continents, Europe, Asia and Africa, divided by the Mediterranean sea and the rivers Nile and Don. East (not north, as on modern maps) was at the top.

world invented by a science-fiction writer than a real country. Everyone agreed it was a land of fantastic riches, inhabited by extraordinary creatures. There were men with dogs' heads, men with one eye in the middle of their foreheads, headless men with their faces on their chests, and giant ants that stored gold in their nests. Strange monsters lived in the seas, too, and many a sailor swore that he had seen a long-haired mermaid frolicking in the waves.

Most of these extraordinary creatures were probably born in the works of writers whose travels took place in their own imaginations, not in any real country; but others had their origin in fact. The story of dog-headed men, for example, may have come from some ancient account of a certain type of baboon, which has a very dog-like head. And the enchanting mermaid of the sailors' stories was probably a flattering report of either a walrus in northern seas, or a sea-cow in warmer waters.

At least mermaids were harmless. The open sea held terrors. Some men believed that if a ship sailed far enough across the ocean to the west, she would reach the edge of the world and fall off into Hell. Some thought that if they journeyed too far south, towards the equator, they would be fried by the tropical sun. Others, with more reason, believed that the sun would turn them black, like the people who lived in tropical Africa.

There were dozens of such tales, but in the 15th century educated men no longer believed them. They knew that the Earth was round, and they knew that it contained three great continents: Europe, Asia and Africa. On the other hand, they believed a fourth continent, as large as Europe and Asia combined, existed in the southern hemisphere. They knew nothing of North or South America, or of the Pacific Ocean.

In spite of these huge mistakes, they had some idea of the world as it really is. It was time for the ships to sail, to find out the true shape of the oceans and the continents.

**Above: These 'men' appeared in an edition of Marco Polo's famous book of *Travels*, largely treated as a fairy tale.
When so little was known about the real world, it was easy to invent creatures which were supposed to live in mysterious and far-distant lands.**

**Top and left: There is even a dragon here as well as a dog-headed man. Angry whales were shown engulfing whole ships.**

# The Pathfinders

When a captain sails his ship out of sight of land, he must have some method of navigation to calculate his position and follow his course. Nature helps him in several ways. For example, the sun rises in the east and sets in the west. So, if the dawn appears on the left of a ship, she must be sailing roughly south. At night a more accurate guide is the Pole Star. Unlike the sun, the Pole Star does not change its position by the hour: it remains constantly in the north. As you go farther north, the Pole Star climbs higher in the sky; as you go south, it sinks lower. The Pole Star disappears near the equator, and navigators in the southern hemisphere had to find new stars to guide them there. By marking north, the Pole Star indicates a ship's *direction*; by its height in the sky it also indicates her *position* between the North Pole and the Equator.

Early navigators made their way from place to place by *dead reckoning*. This was really the same as intelligent guesswork. They relied on their own experience of winds, currents, and so on, to estimate the distance and direction the ship had traveled since leaving port. The ship's speed could be roughly

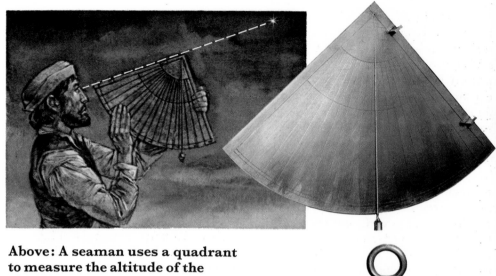

**Above: A seaman uses a quadrant to measure the altitude of the Pole Star.**

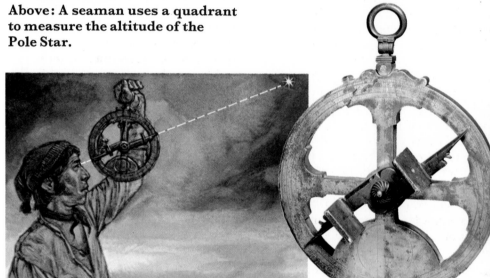

**Below: To use a cross-staff, the staff was lined up with the horizon and the sliding cross-**

piece with the star. This cross-staff has several cross-pieces for measuring different angles.

**Above: The astrolabe had no plumb-line so was easier to use in a ship at sea than a quadrant.**

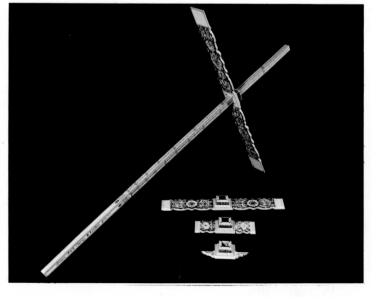

calculated by a *log line*. This line had knots spaced out along it, and was thrown out behind the ship. The *rate of knots* was measured by *sand-glasses*, primitive time-keepers like modern egg-timers. Dead reckoning was fine for short voyages on well-known routes, but for a long voyage in an unexplored ocean it was almost useless. More accurate methods were needed. Though instruments such as telescopes and accurate clocks had not yet been invented, European navigators in the 15th century did have some scientific instruments to help them find their way. The *compass* was the most important. A compass is a piece of magnetic iron which, if allowed to move freely, always points north. The early ship's compass was an iron needle, magnetized by a *lodestone* on a small piece of wood floating in a bowl of water. This early compass was soon replaced by a brass instrument in which the magnetic needle swung around an upright pin. The compass was enclosed in a box, and an oil lamp placed beside it so the steersman could see it on a cloudy night when no stars were visible.

These early compasses were not completely reliable. No one knew that magnetic north is not the same as true north, or that its position varies from year to year. This was only a small problem. A good navigator such as the famous Christopher Columbus could follow a course fairly well. But the navigator also had to be able to calculate his position in terms of *latitude* (distance from north to south) and *longitude* (distance from east to west).

Latitude could be measured roughly by eye. This was done by estimating the height of the Pole Star above the horizon. Instruments were available for more exact measurement. One of the earliest was the *quadrant*, the more accurate ancestor of the *sextant* used today. The quadrant was a quarter-circle, with degrees from 0° to 90° marked around its curved edge. One of the straight edges had tiny holes, or sights, at each end, and a plumb-line hung from the topmost point. The navigator lined up the sights on the star. The plumb-line, which hung straight down, would then be crossing the curved edge at a particular point. This indicated the height of the star in degrees, which gave the latitude.

Another way of determining latitude was to measure the altitude of the sun at noon. As you cannot possibly squint through a sight at the sun, seamen used an *astrolabe*. The seaman's astrolabe was a simple wooden disc with degrees marked around the edge, and a rotating arm with small holes at either end. The disc was hung vertically from a ring. Then the arm was moved until the sunlight, shining through the hole at one end, fell on the hole at the other. The arm then indicated the altitude on the scale marked around the edge of the disc.

Both of these instruments had one drawback. This was that the movement of the ship made it very difficult to take an accurate measurement at sea. The *cross-staff* got over that problem, but the cross-staff was a 16th-century invention.

In spite of the difficulties, 15th-century measurements of latitude were usually not far out. Longitude was more of a problem. It is impossible to measure longitude exactly without an accurate clock, and a clock which would keep perfect time at sea—the *chronometer*—was not invented until the 18th century. Without it, measurement of longitude depended on an estimate of distance sailed. On a voyage of hundreds of miles such estimates could go badly astray.

**Right: Using a compass in a ship in the 14th century.**

**Below: The circular card on a compass was marked with 32 or 64 'points' (later 360 degrees).**

# The Discoverers' Ships

Cog

Double-masted Lateen

The voyages of discovery that began in the 15th century were all made in sailing ships. At that time there were many different types of ship in the world which could have made ocean crossings. Some of the large Chinese and Arab ships could have made these voyages but, because neither the Chinese nor the Arabs had any special reason to set out on voyages of discovery, they never did. (Although the Chinese did visit East Africa early in the 15th century, before the Europeans arrived.)

In Europe, each port in every country had its own tradition of shipbuilding. No two ships were exactly alike. However, most sea-going ships belonged to one of two types. The northern type was seen in the coastal waters of Europe, and the southern type in the Mediterranean. The two types developed separately, and neither one had changed very much in hundreds of years. But in the 15th century the Portuguese, soon followed by other nations, developed a new type of vessel. This had the best features of both northern and southern shipbuilding traditions.

The two main differences between the northern ship and the ship of the Mediterranean were in their *rig* (type of sails) and in the method of building the hull. The northern ship, called a *cog*, was *square-rigged*. It had a single, square sail on a central mast. The Mediterranean ship was *lateen-rigged*, with big triangular sails on two or three masts. The advantage of a square sail is that the ship sails well before the wind. It is not so good when the wind is *on the beam* (blowing from the side) and it is very poor for sailing into the wind, unlike the lateen-rigged vessel. Mediterranean ships sailed well when the wind was on the beam, but were unstable when the wind came from behind.

Northern ships were *clinker-built*. This means each plank of the hull overlapped the next one, like slates on a roof. Mediterranean ships were *carvel-built*: the planks of the hull, fitted edge to edge, were nailed on to the frame. Previously, the hull of a carvel-built ship had been built first and the frame fitted afterwards. The new method, used in northern Europe before 1460, meant the ship

was stronger. In addition, a carvel hull could be larger, and its clean lines made it move easily through the water.

The type of vessel in which the Portuguese made the first voyages of discovery was called a *caravel*. The first caravels were lateen-rigged. But experience soon showed that, for ocean voyages, it was best to have square sails on the *fore* and *main* masts, and a lateen sail on the *mizzen* (the mast at the stern). They were carvel-built in the Mediterranean tradition, but some features of the hull showed the influence of northern shipbuilding. For example, they had a strong, straight *keel* or backbone like that of the cog, instead of the curved keel of most Mediterranean ships. They were slimmer than the rather dumpy cog. The planks of the hull bent round to meet at a single post at the stern, as they did at the bow, though the flat, *transom* stern appeared on many ships before the end of the 15th century.

Although the caravel was first developed as a coastal vessel, it proved excellent for long ocean voyages. Its

Caravel

sailing ability was so good that it was never at the mercy of contrary winds. It must have been a safe ship, too, since we hear of few caravels being wrecked on voyages of discovery.

Caravels came in many shapes and sizes, but all of them would seem very small today. Most were less than 100 feet long with a single deck and a small *poop* (a raised section at the stern) containing the captain's cabin.

But long voyages really required bigger ships, with more space for cargo and supplies and better quarters for the crew. Ferdinand Magellan could not have sailed around the world in a caravel. Many explorers used other ships of the *carrack* type. These were similar in rig to the later caravels but larger, more strongly built, with larger 'castles' at the bow and at the stern. By the end of the 15th century caravels were already going out of fashion. They had served their purpose. The combination of shipbuilding traditions of northern and southern Europe which had produced the caravel began a new line of sailing ships. This led to the great 19th-century clipper ships.

**Above: The cog, on the left, was a simple, rather tubby ship of the late Middle Ages in northern Europe. During the same period, double-masted lateens, like the one in the center, sailed in the Mediterranean. The caravel on the right was the final stage in the development of the lateen-rigged Mediterranean type of ship.**

**Below: A fleet of 16th-century Portuguese ships of the carrack type, in common use at that time.**

# Shipbuilding

The first requirement for building ships was a forest. Ships were built entirely of wood, and used up a great deal of it. A large warship built in the early 16th century contained nearly 2,000 tons of timber, or about 2,000 oak trees. Smaller ships took less but, to obtain the wood for four or five, about 200 acres of forest would have to be cut down. The best available wood for ships is oak, but unfortunately this is slow-growing. Faster-growing trees are less good as their wood splits more easily. Even in a country like England, which had many forests, suitable timber was becoming scarce in the 16th century.

Ships were built close to the water and, if possible, close to the forest. The *shipwrights* (shipbuilders), carpenters and sawyers were sent to select trees to be cut down. Tall, straight-growing trees were especially valuable for masts, and were often marked months or years before they were needed. Blacksmiths set up their forges in the shipyard to make nails and bolts, and other workmen began to make cables and ropes of hemp. The ship's guns and anchors were ordered from the nearest iron foundry.

There was little written material on shipbuilding before the late 17th century. The shipwright, like other craftsmen, kept his skills a secret (another word for *craft* was *mystery*, or something that is secret or hidden). Shipbuilding was often a family business, each shipwright teaching the trade to his son.

In spite of the secrecy, some kind of plan of the ship was made, though it was not followed as exactly as a modern builder follows his *blueprint* (detailed plan). One difficulty was that the weight of the ship was never known until it was finished. Shipwrights often made a model of the ship first, and sometimes drew a plan, cutting the timbers to fit.

The backbone of the ship was the *keel*, which was laid on wooden blocks. The *stem* and *stern posts* were fastened at either end. The floor timbers were laid across the keel and the *keelson*, a kind of internal keel, bolted through

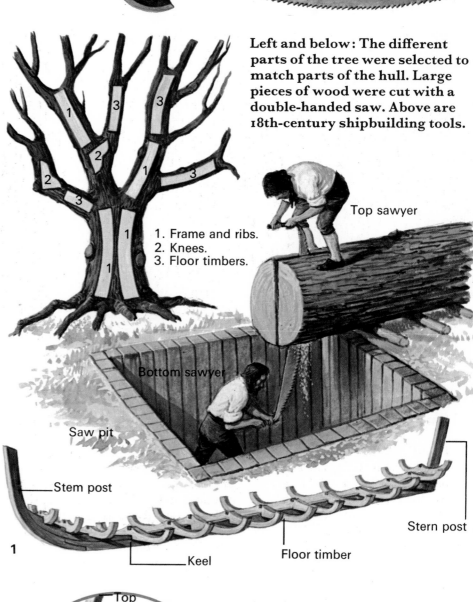

Axe

Double-handed saw

**Left and below: The different parts of the tree were selected to match parts of the hull. Large pieces of wood were cut with a double-handed saw. Above are 18th-century shipbuilding tools.**

1. Frame and ribs.
2. Knees.
3. Floor timbers.

Top sawyer

Bottom sawyer

Saw pit

Stem post

1

Keel

Floor timber

Stern post

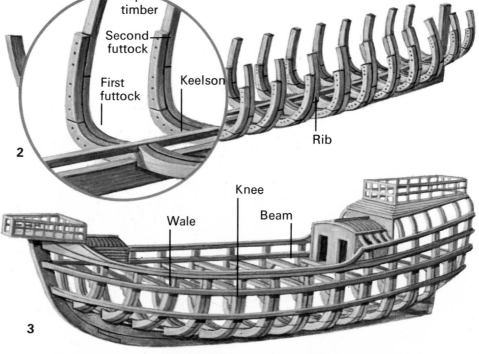

Top timber

Second futtock

First futtock

Keelson

Rib

2

Wale

Knee

Beam

3

Adze  Augers  Brace  Hammer  Caulking iron

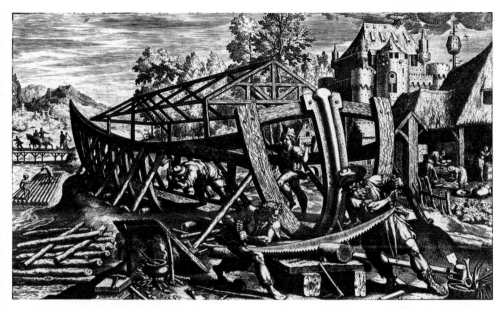

**Above: This engraving of the building of Noah's Ark shows early 16th-century shipbuilding methods. Tools being used include saw, hammer and adze, used for shaping timbers.**

**Left: Building the hull:**
**1. The keel was laid first, stem and stern posts fitted, and the floor timbers bolted to the keel; 2. The keelson was fitted above the keel on top of the floor timbers and the *ribs* added, built up with *futtocks* and *top***

*timbers;* **3. The ribs were then bound together with long pieces called *wales*, running from stem to stern. *Beams* were laid across, between the ribs, and secured to them by brackets or *knees*. Finally, the planks were fastened to the outside of the hull, the deck was laid and superstructures erected at bow and stern; 4. After the seams had been caulked, the hull was ready to be launched. The final stage, raising or 'stepping' the masts, was done when the hull was afloat.**

the top of the floor timbers to the keel with large iron or wooden bolts. The curved timbers forming the ribs of the hull came next. They were placed closer together near the middle of the hull, where the danger of breaking apart was greatest. Each frame was built so that adjoining pieces overlapped to make a strong joint. Shipwrights used to keep a look-out for naturally-curved pieces of timber which would be much stronger than wood cut across the grain to make the curved parts of the ship.

Scaffolding was raised around the growing hull for easier working and planks were fastened to the timbers, both inside and out. The planks, which had to be bent around to the stem and stern posts, could be up to 6 ins thick. The total thickness of the walls of the hull could be more than 20 ins. The planks were fixed to the outside of the hull by wooden pegs. These pegs were made secure with wedges of wood hammered in. *Oakum*—fibers from old ropes—was hammered into the seams between the planks to prevent leaks. The seams and the outside of the hull were then coated with hot pitch. This kept the hull watertight, though it did not prevent *sea worms* from eating into the timbers after weeks at sea.

The finished hull was launched, which meant very heavy work with winches and levers. It was then moored alongside a *hulk* (an old ship) used as a working platform or alongside a quay. From there all the masts and rigging were put in place. Before the sails were set, the hull had to be *ballasted* (made steady) with gravel to prevent it from rolling over. Once the sails were set, the ship would be very top-heavy.

Some ships were beautifully decorated, with carved wooden figures painted with gold leaf, and ornamental panels on the sides. The ships of the discoverers were plainer than the bigger and grander ships of the time. But they, too, carried very long decorative pennants and had painted sails.

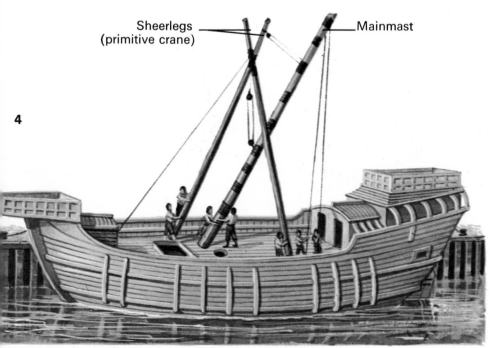

Sheerlegs (primitive crane)  Mainmast

4

# Preparing for a Voyage

Discoverers did not set sail without some idea of where they were going. They did not always find what they expected, and sometimes the country they were seeking did not even exist. But they always had a destination in mind and a plan of how to get there. More often than not, of course, they had to change their plans before the voyage was over.

A captain could not sail off into the blue when he liked. He had to get the permission and support of the royal government of his country. Without these he had neither the money nor the influence to hire ships and crews. Some of the money might be invested by merchants hoping to make a profit from future trade with new-discovered lands, but most of the great voyages of discovery were made in the direct service of the government.

Ships were not chosen specially for their seaworthiness, or sailors for their experience in voyages of discovery. Someone who saw the ships being prepared for Ferdinand Magellan's voyage around the world thought they looked so old and battered they would hardly reach the harbor mouth, never mind the Pacific Ocean. In addition, some of the members of the expedition had never made a long sea voyage before.

Ships' crews were large, because many men were needed to handle sails, and because it was more than likely that some would die during the voyage. The captain was not always a seaman himself. He might be a soldier or a merchant, or a gentleman of the court with a taste for adventure. If so, navigation was the responsibility of the *first mate*, or *pilot*. The *boatswain* was in charge of the ship's gear, including the sails, rigging, and so on, and the *steward* was in charge of the stores. Below them, the most important members of the crew were craftsmen with special skills: sail-makers, carpenters and *coopers* (barrel-makers). *Caulkers* kept the ship watertight and looked after the pumps. Below them were ordinary seamen and one or two ship's boys, or *gromets*, usually aged about 14.

Some of the seamen might be rough fellows, quick to mutiny, but they were very skillful, practical men. They could convert a lateen sail into a square sail, or install a new rudder in the midst of a stormy sea. More than once, when a ship was wrecked on a distant coast, her crew managed to build a new vessel from the wreckage of the old, and sailed safely home.

One craftsman missing from the crew on early voyages of discovery was the ship's cook. The crew took it in

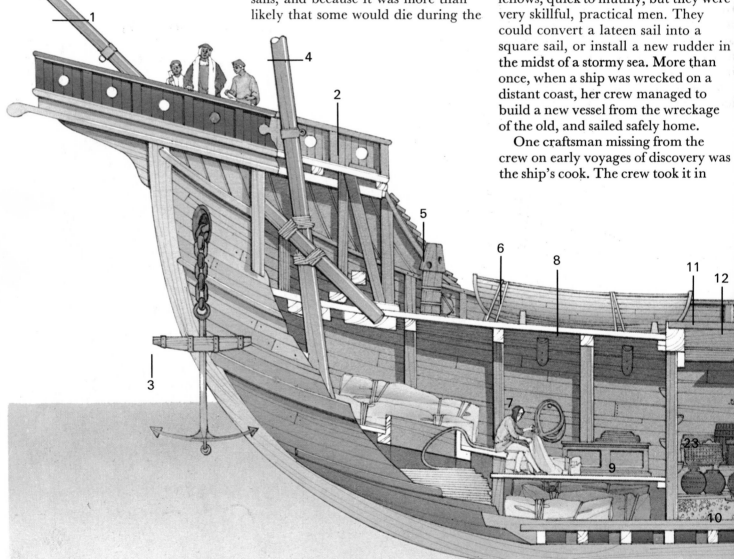

urns to cook, for not a great deal of ooking was done. Food was simple, ecause the provisions suitable for a ong voyage in the 15th century were ew. Meat was preserved by being ickled in salt water. For bread there as *ship's biscuit*—a flat loaf made rom flour with as little water as ossible, and baked very slowly until t was hard. It lasted a long time, hough by the end of a long voyage it ad become a pile of stale crumbs, eaving with black-headed weevils. Old sailors used to say that the weevils vere more nourishing than the iscuit. Cheese and salted fish were ften carried and with luck sailors night catch fresh fish over the side of he ship. Onions and dried beans were he main vegetables. The lack of fresh ruit or vegetables caused a disease alled *scurvy*, which results from ack of vitamin C. Otherwise, the food n board was not much worse than the ood most sailors ate at home.

Drink was a serious problem. Water oes not keep for long in barrels and although ships carried wine as well, that turned sour after weeks at sea. Ships took on water at the latest possible moment. English ships sailing west refilled their barrels in Ireland. Spanish and Portuguese ships stopped at Madeira or the Canary Islands. Fresh water was the first thing to look for when a ship reached land.

These little, overcrowded ships had to find space somewhere for a variety of other objects that might be needed: lamps, tools, weapons (often including cannon), cloth and other trade goods, spare sails, spars, anchors, ropes, canvas, and so on. Some aristocratic captains took fine silverware, splendid clothes, and even musical instruments and a library of books.

**1. Bowsprit; 2. Forecastle; 3. Anchor; 4. Foremast; 5. Movable capstan; 6. Ship's boat; 7. Sailmaker; 8. Main deck; 9. Chest; 10. Ballast; 11. Bulwark; 12. Hatch; 13. Mainmast; 14. Ladder; 15. Mizzen-mast; 16. Quarter-deck; 17. Cabin for officers of ship's company; 18. Captain's cabin; 19. Captain's bunk; 20. Poop; 21. Tiller; 22. Rudder; 23. Ship's stores included all materials for repairing ship, eg sailcloth, rope. Casks, jars, baskets, sacks held water, wine, oil, flour, bacon, vinegar, peas, beans, dried fish, rice, honey, cheese and raisins.**

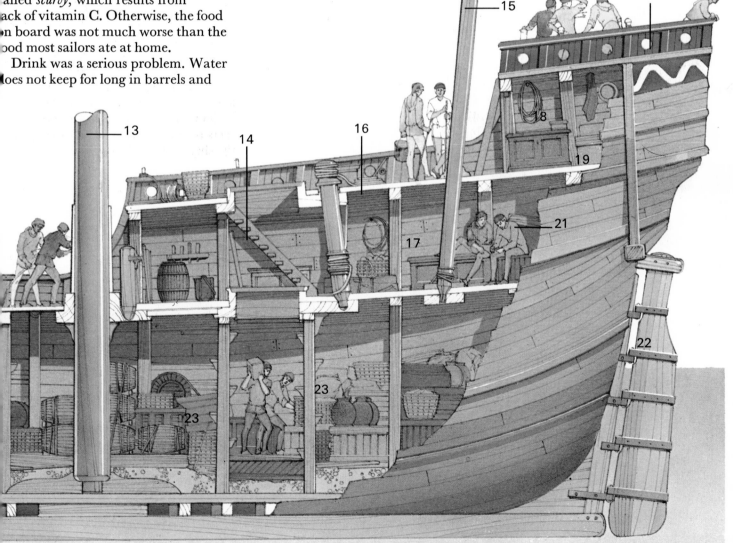

# The Caravels Sail South

The first Europeans to set out on voyages of discovery were the Portuguese. Although Portugal was a small, rather poor country, its position on the south-west corner of Europe made it a good starting-place.

In the 14th century the Portuguese had at last succeeded in driving out the Moors, a Muslim people who had controlled part of Portugal and Spain for several centuries. In 1415 they carried the war into the enemy camp by capturing the Moorish port of Ceuta, in North Africa. Soon afterwards they began their voyages to the south, down the coast of Morocco. They hoped to find a way around the North African Muslims so they could join up with a Christian king, Prester John. He did not exist, but the origin of the legend may have come from the Christian kingdom of Ethiopia, in north-east Africa.

The Portuguese had other reasons for their southward exploration. They hoped to find a sea route to India and the Far East. They could buy luxury goods like silver and spices there since the old trade routes overland had been blocked by another Muslim nation, the Ottoman Turks. They also hoped to find gold. Since they had captured Ceuta they had heard stories of gold mines beyond the Sahara, in West Africa.

The man chiefly responsible for sending out the first caravels was Prince Henry (later called the 'Navigator'), younger son of King John I of Portugal. Prince Henry's captains were unwilling to sail farther than Cape Bojador, a grim red cliff south of Morocco, because they feared they would be unable to get home again; but he scoffed at their fears. How could they know dangers lay beyond the Cape when no one had been to find out?

At last, in 1434, Gil Eannes rounded Cape Bojador. He brought back wild flowers, unknown in Portugal, to prove he had visited a new country. After that ships began to go farther. Time passed, Prince Henry grew old

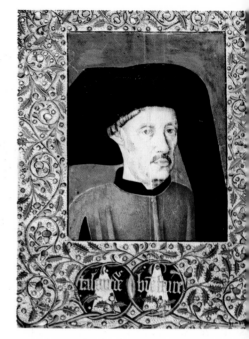

**Above and below: Prince Henry the Navigator was the force behind the Portuguese exploration of the coast of Africa, which began about 1420 with cautious voyages to Morocco. By 1483, when Diogo Cão arrived at the mouth of the River Zaire, all these places had been mapped.**

**Left: Sighting land was always a cause of excitement and meant fresh supplies for the crew.**

EARLY VOYAGES

Lagos

Cape Bojador

N

AFRICA

El Mina

R. Zaire

ATLANTIC OCEAN

Walvis Bay

Cape of Good Hope

Cão 1483
Dias 1487

and died, but the caravels pressed on. The Portuguese set up trading posts along the coast of West Africa.

It took a long time to reach the southern tip of Africa. In 1483 Diogo Cão sailed farther south than anyone before, and discovered the mouth of the Congo (now Zaire) River. To mark his discovery, he erected a huge stone pillar there, which he had brought from Portugal. He was welcomed by the Manikongo, the local king. Before returning to Portugal he sailed on, to Cape Cross, about 80 miles north of Walvis Bay.

Four years later a more famous navigator, Bartolomeu Dias, sailed in search of the route to the East. He left Lisbon with two caravels and a supply ship, and followed Diogo Cão's route along the African coastline to Walvis Bay. From there he headed south. Losing sight of land, he turned east to find it again. But it was not there! Dias guessed that he had passed the end of the continent. He turned north and, sure enough, sighted the coast, now running not from north to south but from west to east. The caravels anchored in Mossel Bay.

Dias wanted to follow the coast farther, but his men were grumbling at so long a voyage. So, rather than risk a mutiny, he turned back. On the way home he sighted the southern cape of South Africa which he had missed on the outward voyage. The Portuguese called it the Cape of Good Hope—'good hope' of finding, at last, the way to India.

**Above: The Portuguese built the castle of El Mina ('the Mine') on the Gold Coast (Ghana). Later, the Dutch enlarged it.**

**Right: In Mossel Bay, Bartolomeu Dias and his crew met the Hottentots, whose cattle provided a welcome meal of fresh beef.**

**Below: The fabled 'Prester John'.**

# The Portuguese and the Kongo

Above: An early chart of West Africa showing the coast as far as the Kongo and the castle of El Mina.

Left: A carved wooden animal mask from the Kongo area.

Right: Diogo Cão and his crew first met a local chief and his tribe when they landed on the left bank of the River Zaire. Later, they were to meet the overlord, the Manikongo.

The Portuguese in West Africa were interested in trade rather than exploration. They set up trading posts and forts on the coasts, but never advanced far inland. In one or two places they tried to settle small colonies, but all of them failed. This was partly because the Africans, while willing to trade with Europeans, did not want them settling on their land.

The intentions of the Portuguese government towards the Africans were good. The government wanted treaties of friendship and trade with African rulers and, if possible, to convert the people to Christianity. Unfortunately, these good intentions were wrecked by the greed of individual men. Many Portuguese who went out to Africa were rough characters, even near-criminals, whose one idea was to make money for themselves. They found that the most profitable trade in West Africa was not in spices, ivory or copper, but in slaves. Friendly contact with the

Africans in the early years soon turned into suspicion and hostility; once-peaceful villages became the scenes of robbery, kidnapping and war.

The way in which Portuguese relations with the Africans turned from friendly co-operation to brutal exploitation is shown in the sad story of the Kongo kingdom.

This story started in 1483 when Diogo Cão discovered the mouth of the Zaire River. It was not hard to find, for the muddy waters of the great river turned the sea brown far out of sight of land. Landing on the left bank, the Portuguese were greeted by a surprised but friendly chief. Cão took four Africans from the court of the Manikongo, the Portuguese name for the supreme ruler. In exchange, he left four of his men behind at the chief's court.

The Kongo kingdom seemed a promising and exciting discovery. King John II hoped that the Zaire River would provide a route into the

interior, leading to the kingdom of Prester John. The four Africans were treated as honored ambassadors, and in 1485 Diogo Cão took them back to Kongo loaded with expensive presents for the Manikongo.

The kingdom which the Portuguese discovered consisted of five or six provinces, each with its own ruler who recognized the Manikongo as overlord. The Kongo people had taken over the area about 100 years before. They had a reputation as clever blacksmiths, whose craft was treated with superstitious awe by all Africans. Smiths still held a high position in Kongo society. They were also great hunters and warriors, and had gained power over the inhabitants of the country by their victory in war.

Above: Africans of the Kongo area are still famous for their craftsmanship. This clay figure, studded with nails, was used in religious ceremonies.

The Manikongo himself was as much a god as a king. He was never seen by ordinary people. When he gave an interview he was hidden from view by a curtain, and even his courtiers were not allowed to watch him eat or drink. The prosperity of the kingdom depended on his good health. If he was ill or discontented, then the crops would not grow, or the women would not give birth. The government was carried on by officials whose position depended very much on his favor.

Some aspects of the life of the people were not so different from those of today. They lived in villages of thatched houses with mud walls, and occupied themselves mostly with their crops and cattle. There were

craftsmen such as the smiths and the artists who carved in wood. Trade was carried on with tribes who lived to the north and east. But then there was a slave trade in Kongo, too. Criminals and prisoners-of-war were made slaves, although this was nothing like the huge and horrible trade introduced by the Europeans.

In 1491 Portugal sent priests to convert the people and soldiers to search for the route to Prester John. They received a wonderful welcome from a throng of people singing and playing instruments, who followed them to the city. The Manikongo was baptized a Christian and his sons received a Portuguese education, while Portuguese craftsmen rebuilt the capital city in stone. A peaceful,

friendly, Christian state was being created—or so it seemed.

Within a few years, things began to go wrong. The Portuguese found the temptation of the wealth to be made from the slave trade too strong. When they found a better source of slaves in Angola, to the south, aid to the Manikongo withered away. There were struggles for power in the royal Kongo family, which lead to civil war. Kidnapping between the tribes in the area and the Portuguese increased. The Manikongo appealed to the king of Portugal for help, but none came. In little more than 100 years, the Kongo kingdom was reduced to a few villages around the Portuguese-built San Salvador. Already the churches there were crumbling into ruins.

19

# The Voyage to India

When Bartolomeu Dias returned from the Cape of Good Hope in 1488, the sea route to India lay open. The Portuguese already knew something about the Indian Ocean from travelers who had gone overland to Aden and India, and the voyage of Dias had proved that India could be reached by sea. One large piece of the jigsaw remained, and that was fitted in by Vasco da Gama in 1497-98.

It was a different kind of expedition from the voyages of discovery that had gone before. The Portuguese knew that when they reached India they would have to deal with civilized Muslim merchants who were probably hostile. They would not be dealing with unsophisticated Africans who thought that the Portuguese ships were giant birds and their sailors messengers from another world. The expedition, made up of four ships, was large for those times. It was also well-armed with firearms and cannon. Its commander, da Gama, was not just a ship's captain but a great ambassador.

Leaving Lisbon in July, the ships followed the usual route as far as the Cape Verde Islands. But from there on da Gama took an entirely new course. Instead of following the coast of Africa, as Cão and Dias had done before, he took his fleet on a great southward sweep through the middle of the Atlantic Ocean. This was the course followed by all later ships: it was shorter and took advantage of the prevailing winds. But how or why da Gama chose this course is a mystery. It was certainly a bold plan, for sailors still grew nervous when land was out of sight, and da Gama's men saw no land for 96 days.

By Christmas, da Gama had rounded the Cape, passing the farthest point reached by Dias. He then began to sail up the coast of East Africa. In March he reached Mozambique.

East Africa was a surprise to the Portuguese. In the south they had met only simple Bushmen and Hottentots. At Mozambique, Mombasa and other East African ports, they found a society in some ways as advanced as their own. The people wore fine linen, trimmed with silk and embroidered in gold. They owned fat sheep and cattle and plump chickens, and grew oranges, lemons and pomegranates in their orchards. When the sultan of Mozambique came on board, he was not at all impressed with the goods offered for trade by the Portuguese. He asked for scarlet cloth, but they had none, and he turned up his nose at the alternatives offered. At Mombasa the Portuguese found a prosperous town of stone buildings. The harbor was crammed with vessels of many kinds, from all parts of the Indian Ocean.

Christians were not welcome in these Muslim cities. At Mozambique, after the sultan had departed, da Gama discovered—just in time—a plot to seize his ships. At Mombasa an attempt was made to cut his anchor cables during the night. Probably the aggressive behavior of the Portuguese, who disliked Muslims just as much as the Muslims disliked them, helped to cause this hostility.

Malindi made a pleasant change. The sultan there, seated on a bronze throne under a crimson canopy, offered a friendly welcome. He was

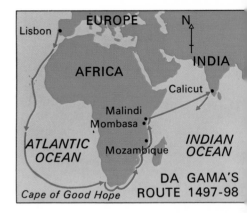

Above: The map shows the route followed by Vasco da Gama on his first voyage to India. The most interesting aspect of the voyage was the southward sweep, far from land, taking advantage of the most favorable winds and currents in the Atlantic.

Right: This tapestry shows Vasco da Gama's reception in Calicut. Reaching India meant a sea route from Europe to Asia had at last been found.

Below: Vasco da Gama receives the blessing of King Manoel before setting out for India.

very interested in the Portuguese ships' guns, which were much more powerful than any weapons in the Indian Ocean. He hoped to make the visitors his allies against the rival city of Mombasa. Da Gama stayed at Malindi for nine days, entertained in rich style by the sultan. He also managed to obtain a pilot to guide him on the final stage of his journey across the Indian Ocean.

Advised by this pilot, who had often made the trip before, the Portuguese crossed the Indian Ocean in 23 days. Giving thanks to God, they dropped anchor in the harbor of Calicut in May 1498. There was no one alive old enough to remember the day when Gil Eannes had returned from Cape Bojador with his strange, wild flowers. But the great enterprise started then had succeeded at last. Portuguese ships had found a sea trade route to India.

# Portuguese Eastern Empire

When Vasco da Gama found the way to India he entered a region of the world new to Europeans, but in many ways no less advanced than Europe. The Portuguese found a thriving international community, and not a primitive wilderness with simple tribes. The Atlantic Ocean was deserted when Christopher Colombus crossed it, but the Indian Ocean was thick with merchant shipping—Arab, Persian, Gujarati and Indonesian. There was even an occasional Chinese junk. When the first Portuguese stepped ashore in India he was greeted by a North African merchant speaking perfect Spanish, who asked him what the devil he was doing there.

In the Indian Ocean there was no need for navigators to map a lonely route through unknown waters. From East Africa to China were large ports, regular shipping lanes and steady trade. The aim of the Portuguese was to control the ports and shipping lanes and seize the trade; they could do that only by force. They were swiftly and surprisingly successful.

The Portuguese had one great advantage over the Muslim traders of the Indian Ocean: their ships were more powerful and better armed. The harbors of Mombasa, Ormuz and Malacca were full of vessels, including large ocean-going ships, but none was built for war.

To control trade the Portuguese first needed key strongholds. The Muslim ports of East Africa—Sofala, Mozambique, Mombasa—soon fell into their hands. In 1510 they captured Goa (in India), the chief center of trade between Persia and Arabia, and India. A year later they took Malacca (in Malaysia), which brought them the trade in spices from Indonesia. It also gave them a headquarters from which they could command the narrow waters between the Indian Ocean and the South China Sea. In 1513 they failed to capture Aden, which commanded the entrance to the Red Sea, but in 1515 they took Ormuz, which gave them mastery of the Persian Gulf. With the small exception of the Red Sea, they were able to dominate all the major routes of the spice trade from their strongholds in Goa, Malacca and Ormuz. They soon gained other trading forts, sometimes by conquest, sometimes by consent of the local rulers, as at Macao, in China.

Their control was not complete, and their advance was often resisted. But the defeat of the Arab-Gujarati fleet in the Indian Ocean (1509) and of a Javanese fleet off Malacca (1513) demonstrated Portuguese supremacy in naval warfare. From then on, merchants in the Indian Ocean had to apply for a license to trade from the Portuguese. Merchant ships found without one were seized or sunk. Meanwhile Portuguese vessels took on shipments of every kind of treasure including gold, slaves, spices and silk from Africa to the Far East.

In the China Sea they met the only opponents who could stop them. The Chinese war junks drove them off, and to gain a foothold in the valuable China trade, the Portuguese had to

**Below: Pepper, being harvested here, was one of the most valuable items of eastern trade.**

**Below right: In Japan, the arrival of Europeans was a popular subject to paint on screens.**

give up their bullying and accept the terms laid down by the Chinese.

The Portuguese achievements in exploration, conquest and trade in the hundred years after Henry the Navigator had died, were astonishing for a small nation. Portugal had only a little over one million inhabitants, about as many as there are in Columbus, Ohio. To create this commercial empire stretching from Lisbon to Japan, brutal methods were necessary. The Portuguese had no respect for non-Christians as human beings. They thought nothing of killing innocent people. They destroyed the large and peaceful system of trade they discovered in the Indian Ocean for their own benefit. Although they produced sincere and saintly missionaries, they also burned mosques and temples, drove away Buddhist priests and Hindu holy men, and made converts to Christianity by force and blackmail. But such savage behavior was not uncommon and not unique to the Portuguese.

**Left: The Portuguese were not welcome in the trade markets of the East. Merchants feared they would lose control of the spice trade, and the Portuguese fought several battles against the ships of Eastern peoples.**

# Columbus

While the Portuguese were creating their trade empire in the East, their Spanish neighbors were building an empire in the west, where a New World had been discovered. The man who discovered the New World for Spain was one of the most famous explorers, Christopher Columbus.

Columbus was an Italian, but he had settled in Portugal as a young man. It was there he became interested in the problem of trade routes to the Far East. The Portuguese were trying to reach Asia by sailing around Africa and across the Indian Ocean, but Columbus had a different idea. He believed that the easiest way to reach the East was by sailing west. As the Earth is round, a ship would sooner or later reach the Far East from the opposite direction; it was only necessary to look at a world globe to see that was possible. Columbus believed that the westward route would be the quickest.

But Columbus's globe did not give a true picture of the world. In the northern hemisphere it showed a single land mass, Europe and Asia, whose eastern and western coasts were separated by the Atlantic Ocean. The existence of the continents of North and South America was unknown and unsuspected. And no one knew there was a Pacific Ocean.

Columbus's map was incorrect in other ways. It made the Earth smaller than it really is by nearly one-third. It also made Asia stretch too far to the east. As a result, the voyage from Europe to Asia appeared fairly simple. Columbus calculated that the distance between the Canary Islands and Japan was 2,400 nautical miles. By coincidence, this is very close to the distance across the Atlantic.

Having decided that the voyage was possible, Columbus's next step was to gain government support. He laid his plan before the Portuguese government, but they turned it down. The Portuguese were not interested in a westward route because their captains were already exploring the route via the Indian Ocean. Columbus turned to other

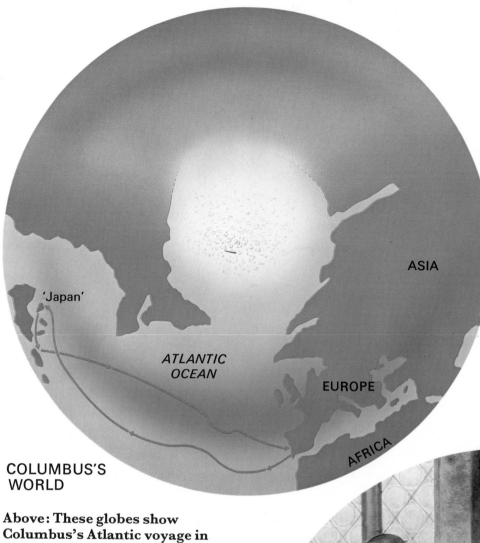

ASIA

'Japan'

ATLANTIC
OCEAN

EUROPE

AFRICA

## COLUMBUS'S WORLD

**Above: These globes show Columbus's Atlantic voyage in 1492. The first one shows the world as Columbus thought it was, and the second the world as it really is.**

**Right: In 1491 Columbus explained his ideas to the Prior of the Abbey of La Rábida, where his son was at school. The Prior persuaded him to wait for Queen Isabella's help.**

governments. His brother Bartholomew tried the kings of England and France, but without success. Meanwhile Christopher went to Spain. He had already been in touch with Queen Isabella, and a Spanish commission had been appointed to study his plan. After long delay, the commissioners reported that the plan was unsound. The ocean, they said, was much larger than Columbus believed, and the voyage would take far longer.

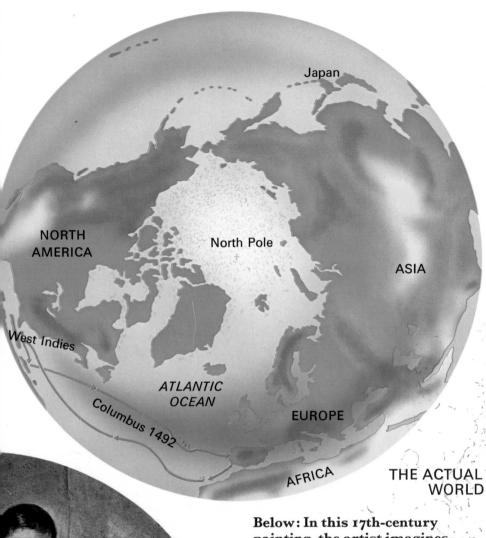

Japan

NORTH
AMERICA

North Pole

ASIA

West Indies

ATLANTIC
OCEAN

Columbus 1492

EUROPE

AFRICA

**THE ACTUAL
WORLD**

**Below: In this 17th-century
painting, the artist imagines
how Columbus presented to the
Spanish King Ferdinand and
Queen Isabella the evidence of his
discovery of what he thought was
the sea route to Asia.**

They were, of course, quite right! Columbus could not agree with them and the Queen sympathetically advised him to wait a while and apply again.

But again the Spanish experts reported unfavorably. Columbus packed his bags, saddled his mule, and prepared to leave the country. He had gone several miles when a messenger from Queen Isabella caught up with him. The Queen had always liked Columbus, and now she said she would pawn the crown jewels, if necessary, to raise enough money for his expedition.

Preparations for the voyage took just over three months. Columbus's flagship was the *Santa Maria*. In the custom of the time she carried a huge square sail on her main mast and a smaller one on the foremast. The mizzen mast, on the high poop at the stern, was lateen-rigged. He also had two caravels, the *Niña*, lateen-rigged, and the square-rigged *Pinta*.

On 3 August 1492 the three ships set sail. In a little over a week, the northerly winds brought them to the Canary Islands, where Columbus had the *Niña* converted to square rig, since she was lagging behind the others. The water casks were refilled and fresh food bought. On 6 September, the ships weighed anchor and set sail due west, heading for unknown waters.

# In Columbus's Ships

It is hard to imagine anything more adventurous than a voyage of discovery. Yet day-to-day life on board Columbus's ships, like life in a space satellite today, was often rather boring. The day was divided into watches, and each watch into half-hours measured by a sand-glass. As soon as the sand trickled down, marking the end of a half-hour, one of the ship's boys would turn it over. Time was checked every day at noon, when the sun lay due south according to the compass.

Columbus's ships made good speed, covering as much as 150 miles a day: a modern yacht does not go much faster. Yet Columbus slightly over-estimated his speed. The result was that he calculated his position at the end of his voyage a little farther west than it was. He sailed along a *line of latitude*—that is due east or due west—as navigators always did when possible, and with a following wind. This meant that the actual sailing of the ship, including manning the sails and navigating the course, was not particularly difficult.

A sailor's life is always hard, but a modern sailor would certainly have found Columbus's ships very uncomfortable. A sailor then could never be certain of getting a hot meal. Food was cooked in a box, bedded in sand to stop sparks causing a fire, on the open deck. Although the fire was protected by a hood, it was impossible to do much cooking in stormy weather. The food was dull, as nearly everything was dried or salted, but enough—if the voyage was not too long.

There were no bathrooms or lavatories, and no one took his boots off at night. The captain had a wooden bunk in his little cabin, but the crew slept where and how they could. In fine weather they would lie on the open deck, but if it was raining they had to find a corner among the cargo and ballast in the hold. In the West Indies, Columbus noticed the natives used hammocks slung between two trees. Soon afterwards, hammocks were introduced to European ships, and made life less uncomfortable.

In Columbus's day, religion had a powerful hold on people. Each exploring voyage was, among other things, a missionary expedition, since every man believed it was his duty to spread Christianity among non-Christian peoples. God was seldom forgotten even in the ordinary running of the ship. The day began with prayers and a hymn, sung by one of the ship's boys. The sea chanties of the time were often religious songs; the boy who turned the sand-glass at the end of the watch would sing a little song like this:

*The watch is called,*
*The glass floweth.*
*We shall make a good voyage*
*If God willeth.*

There was a religious service in the evening, too, attended by every member of the crew. But, as Columbus himself said, a company of unmusical seamen bawling the words of a Latin chant which they did not understand was hard on the ears!

After a month at sea without sight of land, the crew became restless. Ominous mutterings were heard among those off duty. Then, as often happens when a crowd of strangers are cooped up together, tempers grew short, arguments broke out, and mutiny boiled up. The authority of Columbus himself was weak because he was a foreigner who spoke the language of his men with a strong accent. Fortunately, he was loyally supported by his Spanish captains. But on 9 October he was forced to promise that he would turn back if no land was sighted.

Two days later drifting leaves and branches appeared, a sure sign of land nearby. Soon after midnight the look-out on the *Pinta* yelled out, 'Land!' Sandy cliffs appeared in the distance. When day came the ship found an anchorage, and Columbus stepped ashore on a white coral beach. He gave thanks to God, believing he had found an island of the East Indies. The truth was he had discovered the West Indies. The little island where he landed was one of the Bahamas, now known as Watlings Island.

**Above: In the West Indies Columbus noticed the people slept in hammocks (top left) slung between trees. This idea was adopted in European ships.**

**Below: The 'Indians' meet the Spaniards. Columbus called the people of the Americas 'Indians' because he thought he was in the East Indies. Their peaceful nature made it easy for the Spaniards to make them slaves.**

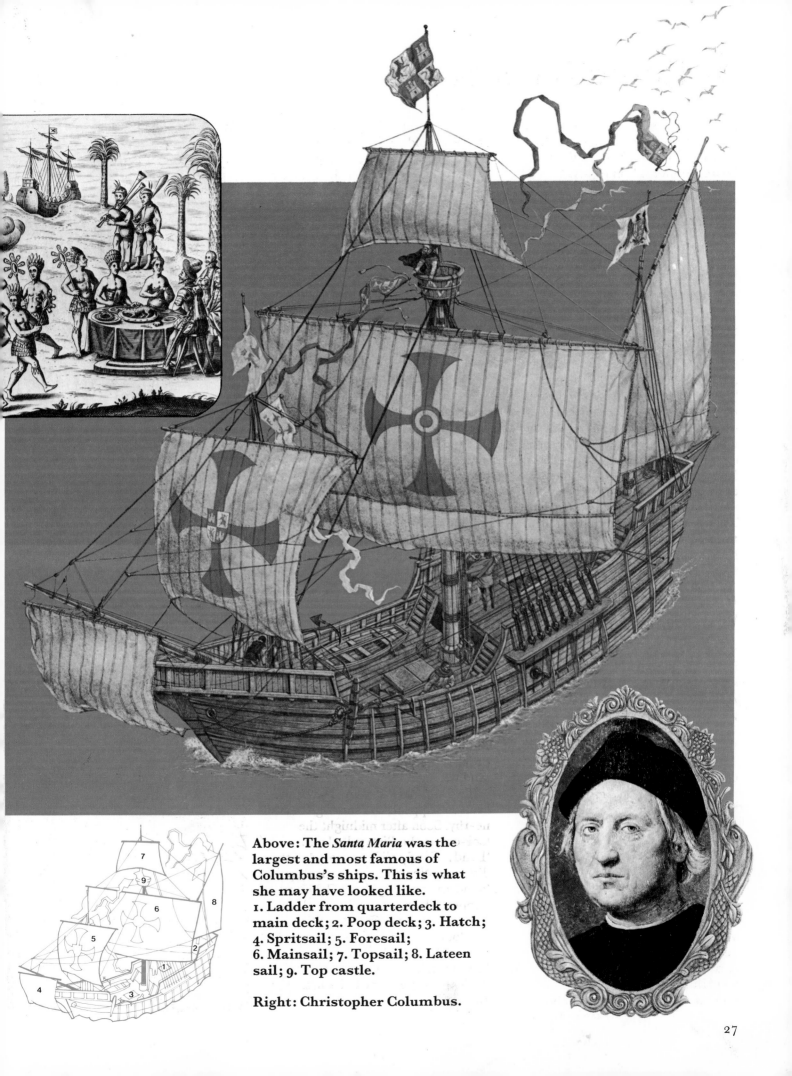

**Above:** The *Santa Maria* was the largest and most famous of Columbus's ships. This is what she may have looked like.
1. Ladder from quarterdeck to main deck; 2. Poop deck; 3. Hatch; 4. Spritsail; 5. Foresail; 6. Mainsail; 7. Topsail; 8. Lateen sail; 9. Top castle.

**Right:** Christopher Columbus.

# Treasures of Montezuma

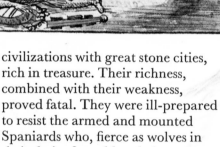

Above and left: The map shows the area controlled by the Aztecs in Mexico and the route taken by Cortés. The Aztecs ruled Central America by their skill in war. Although bloodshed was commonplace, they found enjoyment in music and flowers.

Right: The Aztec ruler carried by his people.

Like the Portuguese in their eastern exploration, the Spaniards discovered new societies in the west. But the people of North and South America were more foreign to Europeans than the people of Asia, and their technology was far less advanced. The Asians were surprised by the power of Portuguese ships and guns, but at least they knew what these things were. The people of the New World had never heard a gun fired, nor seen a sailing ship. They had no metal tools, no plows or carts (they had never invented the wheel), and they had never seen a horse. Some of them had developed wealthy, complicated civilizations with great stone cities, rich in treasure. Their richness, combined with their weakness, proved fatal. They were ill-prepared to resist the armed and mounted Spaniards who, fierce as wolves in their desire for gold and glory, descended upon them in the years after Columbus's discovery.

The Spaniards first settled in the West Indies, cruelly killing and enslaving the natives in thousands. In 1519 the Spanish governor of Cuba sent an expedition, commanded by Hernán Cortés, to investigate rumors of a rich kingdom in Mexico. The purpose of the expedition was to explore, and perhaps seize slaves and treasure. But the ambitious Cortés had bigger ideas. He hoped to gain a kingdom for himself.

Cortés landed at Veracruz and defeated the local people in battle. He learned from them that the rulers of the country were the Aztecs, whose capital was at Tenochtitlán, near the modern Mexico City. The Aztecs were not loved by the people they ruled, and the Spaniards found many allies willing to help them. Otherwise, five hundred ragged Spanish soldiers could never have conquered an empire of five million people.

From Veracruz the Spaniards advanced through steamy jungle, to the high central plain of Mexico. They made their base at Tlaxcala, a city independent of the Aztecs, though often raided by them. Messengers from Montezuma, the Aztec war leader, reached them there. The messages were threatening but Cortés, who was no fool, detected fear lurking behind the threats. Also the greed of his men was whetted by

Left: The Aztecs were skilled at covering objects in turquoise mosaics. This is a breastplate ornament in the form of a double-headed serpent.

the rich presents which the messengers bore. Cortés politely insisted on entering Tenochtitlán, and Montezuma agreed to admit him. It was surprising that the Aztec leader was so trusting, but he may have belived that Hernán Cortés was the Aztec god himself, Quetzalcoatl. According to legend, this god was due to return to earth one day.

The sight of Tenochtitlán satisfied the Spaniards' wildest dreams of treasure. The city was built on islands in a lake, reached by a narrow causeway. Dazzling stone towers climbed towards the sky, gardens rose in terraces from broad straight streets, and canoes paddled back and forth along canals. From the temple where human sacrifices were made to the gods, a flight of 114 steps led down to the ground.

The Spaniards entered the city peacefully, but while Cortés was away his crowd of unruly adventurers quarreled with their hosts, destroying the temples and seizing booty. When Cortés returned, he found his army trapped in a hostile city. Montezuma was stoned to death while trying to pacify his angry people. The Spaniards had to fight their way out along the causeway. Back in Tlaxcala they regrouped and, under Cortés's inspiring leadership, returned to lay siege to Tenochtitlán. They cut off the food supply and knocked down the aqueduct bringing fresh water. They also bombarded the buildings, shoveling the ruins into the lake as they advanced. Their best weapon proved to be smallpox, a disease brought from Europe, which killed the defenders in thousands. At last, twelve years after Cortés had landed at Veracruz, the Aztecs were forced to surrender. Their marvelous city was razed to the ground, and their gold and silver treasures shipped off to Spain.

**Left: When it came to battle, the Spanish soldiers were far outnumbered, but their greatest 'weapon' was their belief that their cause was blessed by God.**

# The Inca Empire

Rumors of golden cities brought Spaniards flocking to the New World. One band of tough, ambitious men, led by Vasco Nunez de Balboa, came from Santo Domingo (now the Dominican Republic) to Central America. They traveled across the narrow isthmus of Darien (Panama), and became the first Europeans to set eyes on the Pacific Ocean.

Among Balboa's band was a former pig-keeper named Francisco Pizarro, who settled down in Darien. He searched for gold, explored the coast, and listened to stories of a great kingdom in the south. When he had collected enough evidence, he went to Spain to ask permission to conquer this unknown kingdom on behalf of the king. Permission was given, Pizarro returned to Darien and, in 1531, set out on his expedition of conquest. He had about 180 men and 27 horses.

The empire of the Incas stretched for half the length of South America. The Incas were a mountain people whose capital city, Cuzco, lay in the Andes of Peru more than 9,000 feet above sea level. Like the Aztecs, the Incas were a conquering race who ruled over many subject nations. Their hereditary ruler, the Inca, was believed to be descended from the god of the sun.

Pizarro's little band sailed down the coast from Darien. When they landed on the Peruvian coast, the Inca empire was involved in civil war. From his base at Quito (now in Ecuador), Atahualpa had just overthrown his half-brother to make himself Inca. That was a stroke of luck for the Spaniards. They went to meet Atahualpa at Cajamarca, exchanging polite messages as they approached and receiving a friendly welcome from the people they met on the way. Pizarro requested a meeting with Atahualpa. The next day the Inca entered the great square of Cajamarca with about 3,000 attendants. Meanwhile, Pizarro had stationed his men in the surrounding buildings.

The interview between the ruler of

Above: Machu Picchu, the most famous and best-preserved of Inca cities, was a great mountain fortress more than 1,500 feet above one of the gorges running through the Andes.

Below: When Atahualpa threw down the Bible, the Spaniards attacked his men with guns and cannon. Many were killed and Atahualpa was captured, later to be strangled by the Spanish.

**Above and right: The Incas made beautiful objects of gold, such as this ceremonial knife, vase in the form of an animal-god, and plate showing the seed time for different crops.**

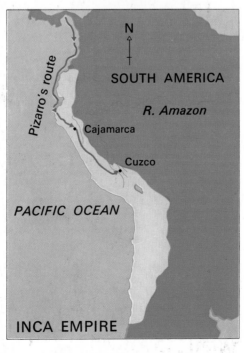

a great empire and the captain of a band of soldiers, carried on through an interpreter, was extraordinary. Pizarro delivered a short lecture on Christianity and demanded that the Inca should declare himself a Christian and a subject of the king of Spain. Not surprisingly he refused, and flung the Bible he had been given on the floor. The Spaniards immediately attacked and the Inca's men, who had few or no weapons, were routed. Pizarro himself grabbed the Inca and, while protecting him from attack, received a wound. Cuzco fell to the Spaniards, and the Inca empire was over, destroyed by a few hundred men.

The gold and silver captured in Cuzco made a rich man of every Spaniard there. But fate was to avenge the Incas, for the victors soon fell to quarreling among themselves. Within a few years, most of them were dead, many (like Pizarro himself) murdered by their own comrades.

Pizarro's men found that movement through the dense forests and steep mountains was hard and dangerous. Nevertheless, they carried out many long journeys of exploration. In 1539 a group led by one of Francisco Pizarro's brothers, Gonzalo, set out to gain land for themselves in the east. They left Quito on Christmas Day and, accompanied by hundreds of Indians, struggled over the mountains in heavy snow. On the other side they found themselves in a wet and empty region. Gonzalo Pizarro sent Francisco de Orellana down one of the rivers to look for food. The current took Orellana's canoe down to a great river, which he named the Amazon. He drifted downstream, and reached the sea, the first man to cross the continent of South America.

Gonzalo Pizarro staggered back to Quito. He had started with 1,000 men. He returned with less than 100.

**Left: By the end of the 15th century, the Inca armies, from their base in the Cuzco valley, had conquered an area extending from Ecuador in the north to Chile.**

# The Discovery of North America

Columbus was not the only man to think of reaching the east by sailing to the west. John Cabot, who was born in Genoa (like Columbus) in 1450, came to England with his family when he was about 30 years old. In 1497, five years after Columbus's voyage, he set out from Bristol in search of a passage to Asia. He sailed with the blessing of King Henry VII and the backing of the Bristol merchants, who hoped they would soon be importing spices from the lands that Cabot would discover.

Cabot had a single ship, the *Matthew*, with a crew of eighteen. Less than 70 feet long, she was tossed about on the broad Atlantic like a cork in a stream. But she was sturdy and well-built, and sailed well before the wind. Cabot knew that Columbus had discovered islands in the west. He meant to be the first to reach the mainland, and his more northerly route would keep him well

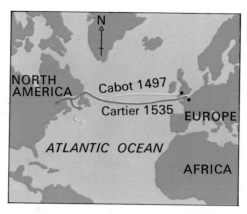

**Above: Routes taken by Cabot and Cartier to North America.**

**Right: Cartier's arrival in Canada: a detail from a world map (here shown upside-down) made after his first voyage.**

**Below: The Lord Mayor of Bristol gives Cabot authority from the king to discover lands. The painting is a modern one.**

away from the Spanish discoveries. Though his distance across the Atlantic was slightly shorter, Cabot's voyage took longer because the winds were less favorable.

On 24 June, after 52 days at sea, land was sighted—a long, quiet coast lined with pine trees. The *Matthew* anchored in a bay. Cabot stepped ashore to claim this 'New Found Land', as he called it, in the name of the king of England. He was convinced that he was on the eastern shore of the Asian mainland. He cruised down the coast a few miles and returned to England to report.

Next year he sailed again. This time he had five ships, loaded with trade goods to exchange for Chinese silks and perfume. But he found no

**Below: Indian tribes along the St Lawrence River lived by fishing and hunting moose. Their canoes were made of bark.**

Chinese, only Indians dressed in skins. It became obvious that he had not found Asia at all and he turned back, a disappointed man.

Though the English followed Cabot's route in order to catch cod off Newfoundland, they lost interest in the New World and made no more discoveries for eighty years. Meanwhile the French, encouraged by King Francis I, made their appearance in North America.

By 1534, when Jacques Cartier sailed there with two ships, the route to Newfoundland was well-known. Although it was early May when he arrived, he had to wait a few days for ice to melt before sailing farther north. He explored the coast of Labrador, which he said was so grim and barren that it might have been the land that God gave to Cain. He sailed southward through the Strait of Belle Isle and was blown by a storm into the Gulf of St Lawrence. He found the mouth of a great river (the St Lawrence) which he hoped would be a sea passage through the New World to Asia. But, as winter was approaching, he decided to postpone his exploration until the next year.

In 1535 he sailed up the St Lawrence to the place where Quebec is now. He made his headquarters there for the winter and, guided by the Indians, took rowing boats to explore the river farther upstream. He got as far as Hochelega, an Indian town and the future site of Montreal.

As a rule, Cartier was on good terms with the Huron and Iroquois Indians, though he was shocked by their poverty. He said that there were no poorer people in the whole world. The Indians thought he came from heaven. They brought their sick for him to heal, while he read the Bible to them sitting under an oak tree. They told him stories of a mysterious kingdom, rich in jewels, up the Ottawa River. He never found this kingdom or a sea passage to Asia. But his journeys took him nearly 1,000 miles from the sea, and he explored more of North America than anyone else until the next century.

# Around the World in 1082 Days

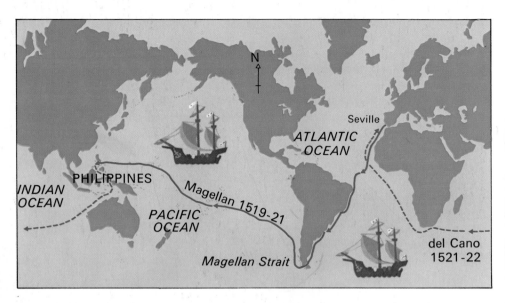

The discovery of a New World on the other side of the Atlantic was a disappointment to those who had hoped to sail direct to Asia. Although the New World contained riches, too, it was an obstacle in the way of the route to the East. That was the object of Magellan's voyage. The Portuguese had already found a south-eastern route, via the Cape of Good Hope. The Spaniards, led by a Portuguese, Ferdinand Magellan, set out to find a route to Asia via the south-west.

In 1494 the Spaniards and the Portuguese had agreed that the undiscovered world should be divided in two. The dividing line was drawn through the middle of the Atlantic. West of the line was the Spanish half, including all the Americas except Brazil, which projected over the line into the Portuguese half. The eastern or Portuguese half included Africa and India. On the other, unknown, side of the world, it was uncertain just where the dividing line ran. Magellan and his supporters realized that if they sailed far enough to the west they would come into the Portuguese half. But they believed that at least some of the Spice Islands were within the Spanish half. Those islands were Magellan's destination.

Magellan's plan was approved by the king of Spain in 1517, and in August 1519 he set sail. He had 260

**Above: Magellan searched for a strait in the far south of South America through to the Far East. It was a very difficult passage. Later, ships found a slightly easier way, farther south around Cape Horn.**

men and five ships. Although only one ship, the *Victoria*, was to return safely, they were well-made merchant vessels, and looked similar to Columbus's ship.

Like Columbus, Magellan was a foreigner in charge of a Spanish expedition, and he also had trouble with his men. Some of the officers did not like him either. That was partly his own fault as he was a prickly character who refused to inform them of his plans.

Matters came to a crisis in cold, grim Patagonia in South America, where the first winter was spent after the long voyage through the Atlantic. Fortunately for Magellan, he was warned that a mutiny was planned. He kept his control by using severe measures. The chief Spanish officer was marooned on that unfriendly shore, and was never seen again. Several men were executed as a warning to the others.

Magellan was confident that he would find a strait in South America which would lead him to the Pacific. Although the entrance is difficult to see even for a captain who knows it is

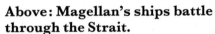

**Above: Magellan's ships battle through the Strait.**

**Left and above left: In Patagonia the explorers saw animals they had never seen before: penguins and guanacos (a type of llama).**

there, Magellan found his strait (now named after him). He led his ships, now reduced to three, through it. The passage was difficult. Ice-topped mountains loomed on either side, and the wind blew like fury dead against the ships. It took 38 days to pass through, though later captains took much longer.

Magellan had no idea of the immense size of the ocean that lay before him. He expected to cross it in a week or two. In fact he was at sea without sighting land for nearly four months. Conditions on the *Victoria* were desperate. The drinking water turned yellow and stinking, and the last of the ship's biscuit was eaten. The starving sailors stripped the leather off the *yards* (spars supporting the sails), soaked it in sea water and toasted it—then ate it. They ate

sawdust from the planks and chased rats—a luxury—in the hold. Many died of scurvy before the ships reached Guam, where at last they got fresh supplies of food and water.

They called at the Ladrones or Thieves' Islands, so named because the local people took everything they could lay their hands on. Then they sailed on to the Philippines. Magellan foolishly became involved in a local tribal war there and was killed during a battle.

Under a new captain, Sebastian del Cano, the *Victoria* reached the Moluccas—the Spice Islands— towards the end of 1521. The Spaniards took on a cargo of cloves and burned one ship, as there were not enough men left to sail her. The captain of the other ship chose to go home the way they had come, but never made it. Meanwhile del Cano took the *Victoria* on across the Indian Ocean, around the Cape of Good Hope, and home through the Atlantic. He reached Seville in September 1522. Only eighteen men, looking more like skeletons, remained alive to tell how they had sailed around the world.

# The North-West Passage

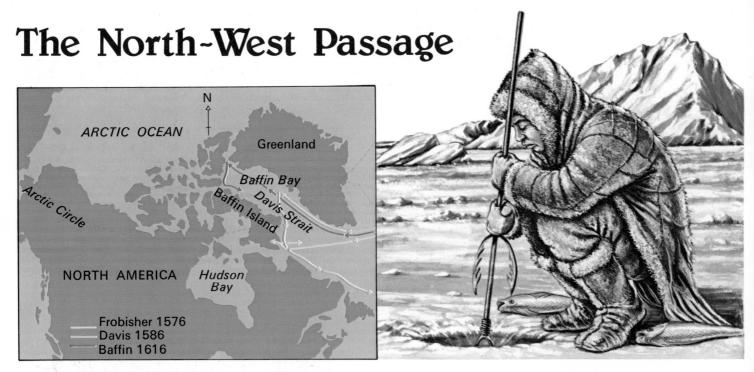

The search for a sea route to the Spice Islands and the Far East had been one of the main reasons for the early European voyages of discovery. This search did not stop when the Americas and the Pacific Ocean were discovered. The Portuguese had discovered a south-east route. The Spaniards, thanks to Magellan, had found a south-west route, though it was so long that few ships used it. The northern countries of Europe searched for a sea passage in the north-east or north-west.

In the north-west, England took the lead. Nothing much came of John Cabot's pioneering voyages in 1497-98 until Martin Frobisher renewed the search in 1576. He sailed in May down the river Thames, passing the palace at Greenwich where Queen Elizabeth stood in the window waving her handkerchief.

After a very cold and stormy crossing, land was sighted and Frobisher sailed into the deep bay in northern Canada now bearing his name. The Inuit or Eskimos there looked like Asians to English eyes, and Frobisher thought he must be sailing along a strait that divided Asia from America.

Next year he sailed again to explore his 'strait' more thoroughly. He made a poor job of it. From his first voyage he had brought back some mineral ore which glittered yellow. Those who saw it believed Frobisher had found

**Above left: The map shows the routes taken by Frobisher, Davis and Baffin in the struggle to find the North-West Passage. There is more than one sea route through Arctic Canada, but parts of these are often heavily choked with**

gold. On his second expedition he was less interested in the North-West Passage than in loading his ships with ore which, in the end, turned out to be completely worthless.

Frobisher's work was continued in the 1580s by John Davis who was interested in every person or thing he saw, not just in getting rich. Frobisher had fired guns at the Eskimos. Davis preferred to play football with them.

Davis sailed around south Greenland, which he called the 'Land of Desolation'. He then went northward through Davis Strait (named after him) as far as the Arctic Circle. He crossed the strait, dodging the pack ice, and explored the bays and inlets of northern Canada, hoping to find the North-West Passage.

One of the inlets that Davis did not investigate was Hudson's Strait. A strong tide runs out of the strait, which probably discouraged Davis from entering. That task was left to the explorer Henry Hudson, after whom the strait is named.

When Hudson, in the *Discovery*, reached Hudson's Strait in 1610, he sailed boldly through, against 'a great

**ice, even in the summer. They are too difficult to be of use as regular shipping lanes.**

**Above: Eskimos hunted fish and seals through holes cut in the ice when the sea was frozen.**

and whirling sea', and found himself in Hudson Bay. He thought he must have found the North-West Passage, and that the coasts of Asia must lie on the other side of the 'sea' he had discovered. As he explored the waters of the bay in wintry fog and ice, his men began to grumble, as seamen always did when far from home. They soon had good cause for complaint for Hudson had left his departure too late. The way home was blocked by ice. He and his men were forced to spend a miserable winter in Hudson Bay, wondering how long the food would last.

The *Discovery* was unable to move until the following summer, but everyone knew there was not enough food for the voyage home. Led by Robert Juet, who had served as mate under Hudson on an earlier voyage, the crew rebelled. They put Hudson, his young son and five loyal sailors into a boat, and set them adrift without food or weapons. It was little better than murder: no trace of them was ever found. As for the mutineers, four were killed soon afterwards in a fight with Eskimos. Robert Juet died

**Above: A modern ice-breaker can force a way through the kind of thick ice that defeated the early explorers in the Arctic.**

**Right: Hudson, his son and a few loyal sailors, were left to die.**

of starvation on the voyage home. Only a few lived to see England again. The brilliant English navigator William Baffin used the *Discovery* in his attempt to find the North-West Passage in 1616. Baffin sailed up Davis Strait but continued up to the northern end of the bay named after him. Unfortunately, Lancaster Sound, which leads through to the North-West Passage, was blocked with ice. Baffin thought there was no way through, and sailed for home.

Although many later captains tried to find a North-West Passage in Arctic Canada, no one succeeded in navigating it by ship until nearly 300 years after Hudson. The Norwegian, Roald Amundsen, forced a way through from the Atlantic to the Pacific, but it took three years, and few ships have managed it since.

# The North-East Passage

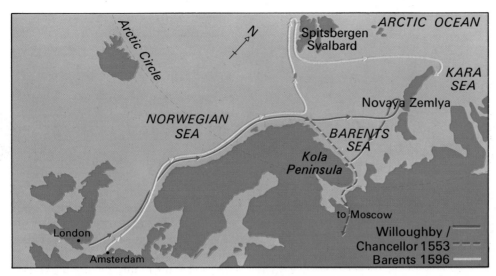

Willoughby /
Chancellor 1553
Barents 1596

No one in the 16th century knew how cold the Arctic is, nor that the Arctic Ocean is mostly ice. Hudson had thought it might be possible to reach the other side of the world by sailing due north, straight over the North Pole. Others tried to go north-east, around Scandinavia and Russia.

In 1553 Sir Hugh Willoughby commanded an expedition in search of this North-East Passage. Sir Hugh was a soldier and a courtier, not a seaman. His second-in-command, Richard Chancellor, was an experienced navigator. But off the coast of Norway the two ships became separated in a storm and Willoughby sailed on alone. He reached Novaya Zemlya, where he turned north but found ice blocking the way. Then he retreated to the Kola Peninsula where he spent the winter. Unfortunately, Willoughby was not prepared for the intense cold, and he and all his men died before spring came.

Meanwhile Chancellor had sailed into the White Sea and landed on the Russian coast. Traveling overland by sledge, he reached the court of Tsar Ivan the Terrible in Moscow. From this meeting, regular trade between England and Russia began. The expedition proved valuable in the end, even though it did not find the North-East Passage.

The Dutch also were interested in the North-East Passage. A well-known pilot, Willem Barents, was one of the leaders of an expedition which

**Above left: Routes taken by Willoughby, Chancellor and Barents in search of the North-East Passage.**

**Above: Sir Hugh Willoughby.**

**Below: Polar bears often travel miles in their search for food.**

**Above: The Dutch house at Ice Haven was ingeniously made. Polar bears and Arctic foxes gave fresh meat and fur.**

**Below: Inside the Dutch house: not *all* home comforts, in spite of hot water, bath (at right), roast fox, oil lamp and clock.**

Fortunately, land was near. The Dutch abandoned the ship and lugged most of the stores across a few miles of ice to a place they called Ice Haven.

For the first time, Europeans succeeded in surviving a winter in the Arctic. They found driftwood on the shore and built a house over 30 feet long and 20 feet wide, with wooden bunks around the walls. It had a fireplace and chimney, and a kind of bath made of wine barrels, where each man bathed once a week. They killed polar bears and walrus for meat, fuel oil, and skins, to keep them warm. Even so, during the long Arctic winter when the sun never rises above the horizon, everything froze solid. When they washed their shirts, they froze like boards. They held them near the fire, but the heat thawed one side only; the other side remained frozen stiff. Their clock stopped, and when they wanted wine they had to chip a piece off a frozen block. Two men died of scurvy; others grew weak and helpless. Barents himself, who was nearly fifty, was very ill by the time spring came.

In May the sea ice began to melt, and the Dutchmen prepared to make their escape in the rowing boats they had saved from the wreck of their ship. Fourteen men huddled in the two boats, as they picked their way among threatening ice-floes. They were over 1,000 miles from safety.

As they rounded the tip of Novaya Zemlya, Barents, lying weakly in the boat, asked to be lifted up so he could take a last look at the 'cursed land' that had held them prisoner. He died later that day. Two others also died, but the rest struggled across the Barents Sea to the Kola Peninsula, where they were rescued by a Dutch ship searching for them.

No one visited Ice Haven again until just over 100 years ago, when Norwegian fishermen rounded the cape and moored there. They found the remains of the Dutchmen's house, their pots and pans, guns and swords, musical instruments, and the old ship's clock which had stopped ticking during that Arctic winter long ago.

managed to reach the Kara Sea in 1594. This was farther east than any ship had sailed before in that latitude. A second attempt, the next year, was unsuccessful, as the ice was worse.

In 1596 Barents sailed again. On this voyage he decided to try to pass to the north of Novaya Zemlya. On the way the Dutch discovered new islands. They named them Spitsbergen or 'pointed mountains' and thought they were part of Greenland. Later these islands became the center of the whaling industry. In mid-July they succeeded in passing the northern cape of Novaya Zemlya, but on the far side the ship was threatened by ice. This crowded in upon her with irresistible force. She could not move, and soon she started to break up.

39

# Siberia

No ship sailed through the North-East Passage, along the icy coast of northern Siberia, until Baron Nordenskiold completed the voyage in the *Vega* in 1878–79. In the meantime, the northern coast had been explored by Russians, traveling sometimes in small boats, sometimes by dog sledge overland.

The man behind this great Arctic effort was Tsar Peter the Great, though he died before it started. The leader he appointed was a Dane, Vitus Bering. But, because of the huge distances involved, Bering was seldom in touch with his subordinates, each of whom explored one section of the coast. Bering's personal task was to travel to Kamchatka and from there to take a ship north to discover if Russia and America were joined.

To reach Kamchatka, Bering had to cross the whole breadth of Russia. Over three years had passed since he set sail in 1728 from St Petersburg (now Leningrad) into the sea now named after him. He passed north through the Bering Strait, proving beyond reasonable doubt that Asia and America were separated. On a

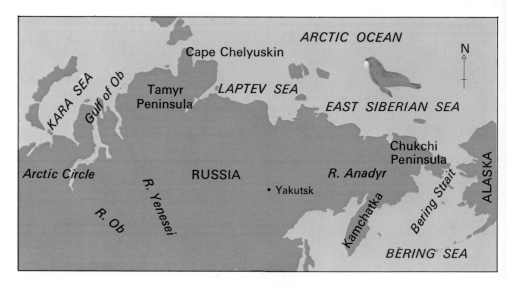

**Above: The coastline of northern Siberia. Tribes such as the Chukchi (right) still live along this forbidding coastline.**

second voyage, in 1741, he reached Alaska, but beset by storms, fog and starvation, he died on Bering Island on the way home.

Meanwhile, the exploration of the northern coast had begun. The first section, from the White Sea to the Gulf of Ob, was completed in 1737, after two previous attempts had failed. That summer happened to be mild, with less ice than usual. The second section from the Ob to the Yenesei

**Left: Chelyuskin and his team, fighting against a blizzard, struggle to reach the cape later named after their leader.**

River, was then conquered. The next objective was the Taymyr Peninsula, which was approached by two groups, one from the west and one from the east. The western group failed to reach it either by sea or by land. All hopes were placed on the eastern group, led by Lieutenant Pronchishev who, surprisingly, took his wife. Both died, and command fell upon the senior surviving officer, Chelyuskin. Chelyuskin decided to travel south to get fresh orders from Bering who at this time, in 1736, was believed to be at Yakutsk on his way east. Unfortunately, when he arrived at Yakutsk, Chelyuskin found Bering had already moved on. He had traveled over 1,000 miles through a bitterly cold country, all in vain.

In 1739, Khariton Laptev was appointed to take over Pronchischev's job of rounding the Taymyr Peninsula. His little boat was crushed by ice in the Laptev Sea, but Laptev struggled back to land and, after dreadful hardships, reached his base.

Beaten by the Arctic seas, Laptev decided to renew the attack by land. He chose the pilot, Chelyuskin, to make the final effort. In the summer of 1742 Chelyuskin finally reached the northernmost cape (now Cape Chelyuskin) of the grim and hostile peninsula.

The fifth and final section of the coast was the hardest of all. There is a story that a Cossack named Dezhnev traveled from the Kolyma River to the Gulf of Anadyr in 1648, but no one is certain whether he went by sea or overland, or whether he went at all. In the 1730s the job was given to Dmitri Laptev, brother of Khariton. At first he made little progress. He

**Above: Vitus Bering had spent nearly 20 years exploring the Siberian coast. He died weakened by his many hardships.**

missed the mild summer of 1737 because, like Chelyuskin, he was searching vainly for Bering for new instructions. Orders eventually reached him to carry on. But because he thought the sea route was impossible, he marched overland with no less than 45 dog teams. A large party was necessary as the local people, the Chukchi, were very hostile to the Russians. With his arrival on the frozen banks of the Anadyr in 1741, the last section was completed. Some parts of the coast were still unexplored, but in 1742 the general outline was known all the way from the White Sea to Kamchatka. It remained for Nordenskiold to prove a ship could sail through the North-East Passage over 100 years later.

# China and Japan

**Above: Marco Polo embarks at Venice for his journey to China.**

In the 13th century, before the Age of Discovery began, the Far East was not completely cut off from Europe. Merchants from Italy occasionally traveled as far as China. The most famous of them was a Venetian named Marco Polo, who entered the service of Kublai Khan, the Tartar emperor of China. Marco Polo remained in the Far East for more than 20 years, visiting Burma, India and Indonesia.

In many ways civilization in the East was far ahead of Europe. In China Marco Polo saw many things familiar to us but strange to him, such as asbestos cloth, coal-burning fires, dishes of porcelain, paper money and

river bridges 300 metres long. A great city like Hangchow, with its pavilions, canals and broad carriageways, made Venice look like 'a dirty village' according to Marco. His description of China was generally truthful, although he often exaggerated. He reported some very tall stories, like the one about the great bird of Madagascar which seized elephants in its talons and dropped them from a great height. His book, which is called *Travels of Marco Polo*, was popular, but it was treated as a typical

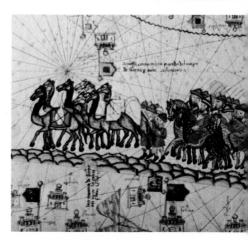

**Above: The civilization of China was much older, and in many ways far in advance of, society in medieval Europe.**

**Above: Father Matteo Ricci.**

**Below: The Polos travel across Asia in an embassy caravan.**

traveler's tale, more fiction than fact.

After Marco Polo, there were few contacts between Europe and China until the Portuguese arrived in the south in the early 16th century. The Ming dynasty, which ruled from Peking, discouraged contact with foreigners, including the Portuguese.

As in other parts of the world, some of the earliest European travelers in the Far East were Roman Catholic missionaries belonging to the order known as the *Jesuits*. A Jesuit from Navarre, called Francis Xavier, was the first man to give an accurate account of Japan. He was delighted with the Japanese, admiring their sense of honor, their courtesy and their moderate way of life. There seemed to him to be little active religion in Japan and therefore, he supposed, the Japanese would be ideal converts to Christianity. But here he ran into a problem. The Japanese were admirers of the great learning and culture of China. They were surprised to find that Jesus Christ was entirely unknown to the wise men of China. Francis Xavier realized that, if he hoped to convert the Japanese, he would have to convert the Chinese first. He set out for China but died before he reached it, in 1552.

In the same year Matteo Ricci was born in Italy. When he grew up he entered the Jesuit order and was sent to Goa, in Portuguese India. There he learned Chinese, and in 1583 gained permission to settle in Canton.

In this way Francis Xavier's dream that Christianity should be preached in China came true.

Father Ricci was a remarkable man and, in many ways, far ahead of his time. He recognized that Chinese civilization was as old and diverse as anything in Europe, and that it would be absurd to try to force Christianity down Chinese throats. The methods that might work among simple people would not work there. So he became a kind of Chinese wise man himself. He dressed in the Chinese way, and built his church in the Chinese style. He won friends by his knowledge of science and geography, and in his teaching he concentrated on the ethical ideals of Christianity rather than its religious doctrines. He even allowed his converts to continue some non-Christian forms of religion, such as ancestor-worship.

Father Ricci's great ambition was to get to Peking, for he knew he could do little without the support of the emperor. In 1600 permission was at last granted: he entered the 'forbidden city' and was well received by the emperor, Wan-Li. He had brought presents, among them a clock which especially delighted the emperor.

Wan-Li agreed to hang a picture of Jesus in the imperial apartments, and from that time Christianity was tolerated in China. The Jesuits made many advances in geographical knowledge, as well as making religious converts.

# Early Discoveries in the Pacific

The business of explorers was not only to discover and chart new lands and seas, but a matter of destroying old myths. As well as adding new features to the map, the discoverers removed old ones. A map of the world drawn in 1800 actually showed less land than one drawn in 1450. This was because voyages of discovery had proved that lands known only from ancient legends did not exist. One example was the island of Atlantis, described in detail by the Greeks, which was believed to lie in the Atlantic. Another was *terra australis*, '*southern land*', a continent shown on many maps in the southern hemisphere.

The belief in a great southern continent was based on logic, of a kind. The ancient Greek geographers knew that the world is a sphere. They knew that the northern hemisphere contains a great land mass, Europe and Asia. From that they reasoned that there must be a similar land mass in the south to keep the earth balanced in space; otherwise, they believed it would topple over. The work of Ptolemy, the Greek geographer who lived in Alexandria in the second century, had a powerful influence on the age of discovery. Maps based on his work showed a land mass in the south, sometimes reaching to the equator. Every new discovery in the Pacific was interpreted as evidence for the existence of *terra australis*.

In 1567 the Spaniards in Peru sent Alvara de Mendaña to discover the 'southern continent' and establish a colony there. His ships crossed the Pacific and eventually returned, after suffering from hurricanes, starvation and mutiny. Their chief discovery was the group of islands called the Solomons, but Mendaña did not calculate their position very accurately. The Pacific is so vast and the difficulties of navigation so great, that no one was able to find the Solomons again for 200 years.

The search was taken up by Mendaña's pilot. This pilot was a brilliant Portuguese navigator called Quiros, who discovered the New Hebrides. One of Quiros's

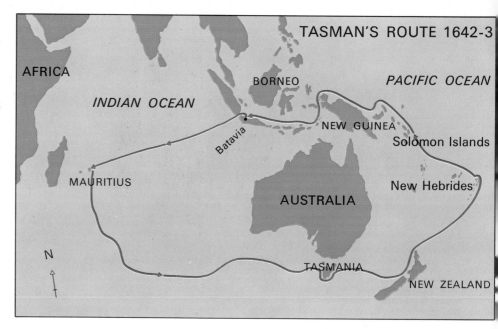

TASMAN'S ROUTE 1642-3

AFRICA
INDIAN OCEAN
BORNEO
PACIFIC OCEAN
Batavia
NEW GUINEA
Solomon Islands
MAURITIUS
AUSTRALIA
New Hebrides
N
TASMANIA
NEW ZEALAND

lieutenants, Torres, was also involved in the search. In 1605 he sailed east-to-west through the strait named after him which divides New Guinea from Australia. He proved that New Guinea was not, as many believed, part of the 'southern continent', but the results of his voyage remained secret, and the point had to be proved again by Cook over a century and a half later.

In the 17th century the Dutch replaced the Spaniards as the leading explorers of the Pacific. They discovered the west coast of Australia, which they called New Holland. Its desert shore and naked people made it seem a poor place. *Terra australis* was supposed to be a rich land, so not everyone was eager to identify New Holland with the missing continent.

The most important Dutch voyage of discovery was commanded by Abel Janszoon Tasman in 1642. From Batavia in Java, he sailed all around Australia—but never once got close enough to sight the mainland. He did discover Tasmania and, continuing eastward, struck the western coast of New Zealand. Here, he believed, was a cape of the 'southern continent'.

In 1615-16 Schouten and Le Maire searched for the 'southern continent', making the first passage south of Cape Horn. In 1721 Roggeveen, sailing farther south,

**Above: The map shows how Tasman sailed around Australia but only sighted Tasmania.**

**Right: The Tasmanians used even simpler tools than the mainland Australian aborigines. Sadly, the Tasmanians are extinct, the last one dying in 1876.**

**Below: Explorers were puzzled by the stone columns on Easter Island, some carved in the form of human statues. Archeologists are still studying them.**

**Above right and right: The aborigines of Australia were a simple, Stone Age people, but had successfully adapted to life in a hard, infertile land.**

discovered Easter Island. These and other voyages made rather large holes in the 'southern continent', but did not end all belief in its existence. One book, published in the 1740s, stated bluntly: 'It is most evident . . . that New Guinea, Carpentaria (northern Queensland), New Holland, Tasmania and the countries discovered by Quiros, make all one continent, from which New Zealand seems to be separated by a strait'. This error was not resolved out until the time of Captain Cook.

# New Zealand and Australia

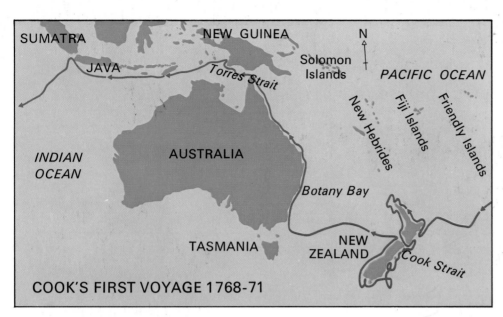

COOK'S FIRST VOYAGE 1768-71

Left: The map shows Cook's exploration of the coastline of New Zealand, and his route along the Great Barrier Reef.

In 1768 Lieutenant James Cook left England in the *Endeavour* bound for the South Pacific. The main purpose of the voyage was to make an observation of the planet Venus as it passed across the sun (which happens only at long, irregular intervals). From such observations in different parts of the world, scientists hoped to calculate the distance of the sun from the Earth. Cook's observation post was to be set up in the newly-discovered island of Tahiti.

The voyage had a second object. After the observation, Cook was instructed to look for the 'southern continent'.

Cook was much better equipped than earlier explorers. He had instruments such as a *reflecting telescope*, a *theodolite*, a new improved *azimuth compass*, and a good timekeeper—the recently invented *chronometer*. His provisions included *sauerkraut* (pickled cabbage), which may have helped keep his 100 men free of scurvy, and 'portable soup', a primitive kind of stock cube.

The *Endeavour's* passengers included a young botanist, Joseph Banks, and a number of animals, including sheep, pigs and chickens. Fresh milk was provided by a goat which had already made one voyage around the world.

The *Endeavour's* crew spent several weeks in Tahiti, a tropical paradise where the people were friendly, the

girls and the scenery beautiful and the food abundant. They observed Venus making its transit, then sailed south, searching for 'mountain peaks' which had been sighted on an earlier voyage. The 'peaks' were probably clouds, for Cook found nothing until he reached the land first discovered by Tasman— New Zealand.

Tasman had trouble with the Maoris and so did Cook. Though anxious not to offend them, he was forced to fire on them in self-defence.

Fortunately, they were more friendly farther north. Cook made friends with them, with the aid of an interpreter from Tahiti whose speech the Maoris understood. Eighty years later an old Maori told how as a small boy he had visited the *Endeavour*, how Cook had patted him on the head and given him an iron nail for his fishing spear. The Englishmen admired the Maoris for their courage. They wrote the first account of Maori life, though in a short stay they could only describe

Above center: A chronometer made by the Yorkshire clockmaker, John Harrison.

Left: Dusky Bay in New Zealand, an inlet charted by Cook.

Above: The Maori war canoes were often highly decorated.

Right: The Maoris decorated themselves with intricate, tattooed designs.

Left: Cook was shocked by human sacrifice in Tahiti, though the victims were usually condemned criminals.

the obvious things, like houses and crops. There was no time to observe the more complicated aspects of their life, like Maori religion and ideas.

In a few months the *Endeavour* sailed around New Zealand's North and South Islands, passing through Cook Strait. It was a masterly survey, and proved without question that New Zealand was not part of any 'southern continent'.

From New Zealand the *Endeavour* sailed towards Tasmania, but she was carried farther north and sighted the Australian mainland near Botany Bay. This place, the future site of the first British settlement, gained its name from the numerous unknown plants that Banks collected there. Sailing north, Cook marked the features of the east coast, which no European had seen before. He then came to the Great Barrier Reef, that dangerous ridge of coral off the coast of Queensland. There the voyage nearly ended in disaster when, in spite of careful work with the *lead* (to measure the depth of water under the ship), the *Endeavour* grounded on a coral spur.

After fifty tons of ballast and the ship's guns were thrown overboard (the guns were recovered in 1969), she floated off, but she was leaking badly. To make her safe, Cook tried *fothering*. A spare sail was filled with old bits of rope and sheep's dung and passed under the ship, like a sling. When pulled tight, the soft material was forced into the holes made by the coral. This temporary repair lasted until she could be safely beached, near the modern Cooktown, and the hull repaired properly.

After passing through Torres Strait and calling at New Guinea (proving it was not joined to Australia), Cook sailed home via the Cape of Good Hope. The *Endeavour* reached Dover in July 1771, nearly three years after she had left England.

# Cook's Pacific

Cook had not proved beyond doubt that the southern continent did not exist. It was obvious though, that it must be far smaller than the old map-makers had believed. In 1772 he sailed on a second voyage of exploration in search of it. His plan was simple. He would simply sail to a far southern latitude and then circle the world. If the continent was there, he would be bound to strike it.

This time he took two ships, the *Resolution* and the *Adventure*. Like the *Endeavour*, they were both former north-country *colliers* (in fact all

**Right: This map of the Pacific shows Captain Cook's last voyage.**

**Below and below right: Breadfruit was the staple diet of South Pacific Islanders. The artist in the *Endeavour*, Sydney Parkinson, painted this plant and also sketched the kangeroo.**

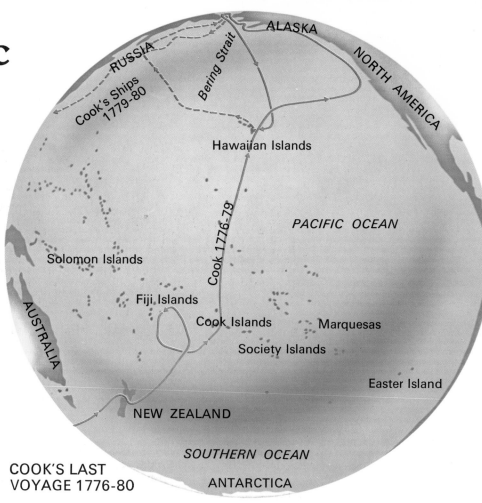

RUSSIA · ALASKA · NORTH AMERICA · Bering Strait · Cook's Ships 1779-80 · Hawaiian Islands · PACIFIC OCEAN · Cook 1776-79 · Solomon Islands · Fiji Islands · Cook Islands · Marquesas · Society Islands · AUSTRALIA · Easter Island · NEW ZEALAND · SOUTHERN OCEAN · ANTARCTICA

COOK'S LAST VOYAGE 1776-80

three were built in the same Whitby shipyard). Banks wanted to go again, but he insisted on a larger ship and more artists and scientists. He also wanted to take his girl-friend, disguised as a man! His demands were refused so he went off to Iceland instead, and another scientist, J. R. Forster, was appointed. Forster was a less agreeable character than Banks, but he did sacrifice his pet dog to make a tasty soup for Cook when he was ill in the Southern Ocean.

At the beginning of 1773 the ships reached the Antarctic Circle south of the Cape of Good Hope. The sails stiffened and the ropes froze as hard as iron bars. Huge flat icebergs drifted past on a grey sea. Ordering extra nips of spirits for all hands, Cook sailed east. The ships became separated, but met again in New Zealand where they spent the winter. The following year they sailed south and east again, crossing the Antarctic Circle at two points but each time forced northward by ice. The third summer Cook passed Cape Horn and completed the third and final section of his circle round the world when he crossed his own route south of the Cape of Good Hope.

The *Resolution* had been farther south than any ship before. New islands had been discovered, but no mainland. Although he came near at several points, Cook never sighted the true southern continent, Antarctica. But the voyage had proved that, if a southern continent

**Above: During Cook's last voyage, in search of the North-West Passage, his men organized hunting parties to shoot walrus.**

**Below: The death of Cook in Hawaii due, it seems, to a misunderstanding, was a tragic end to a great career.**

did exist, it could hardly be any larger than Antarctica actually is.

Cook's third voyage had a different purpose: to seek the North-West Passage. Unlike earlier searchers, he began by seeking the Pacific exit of the passage. He sailed, again in the *Resolution*, via South Africa and New Zealand, and called at some of his favorite stopping places in the Pacific on his way north.

Cruising north with the trade winds, the *Resolution* sailed up the coast of Alaska and entered the Bering Strait. Cook continued north

until forced back by the drifting Arctic ice. In the strait, Cook's men had the exciting experience, denied to Bering when he had entered these waters, of seeing Asia on one side and North America on the other.

In November 1778 Cook made his most important discovery when he came upon the island group known as Hawaii. The Hawaiians spoke, like the Maoris, a version of the same language as the people of Tahiti. Cook was amazed by this evidence of how the Polynesian people had spread themselves over the vast Pacific Ocean at some time in the past. The Europeans were not the only ocean-going race.

The Hawaiians, like the Tahitians, were friendly. Simpler people than the Tahitians, they thought that Cook's men were supernatural creatures, and sang hymns in their honor. This time Cook would let no women on his ships, hoping to prevent the spread of venereal disease which European sailors had inflicted on other Pacific islanders. But trade was brisk—iron nails were exchanged for fresh pork.

Unfortunately, good relations did not last. Quarrels broke out over the theft of one of the ship's boats, guns were fired and a Hawaiian chief killed. Cook, standing at the water's edge, turned to signal to the boats, and was stabbed fatally in the back. Sadly, the ships made their way home, bringing the remains of the greatest of all maritime explorers to their last resting place in Westminster Abbey.

# The Discovery of the World

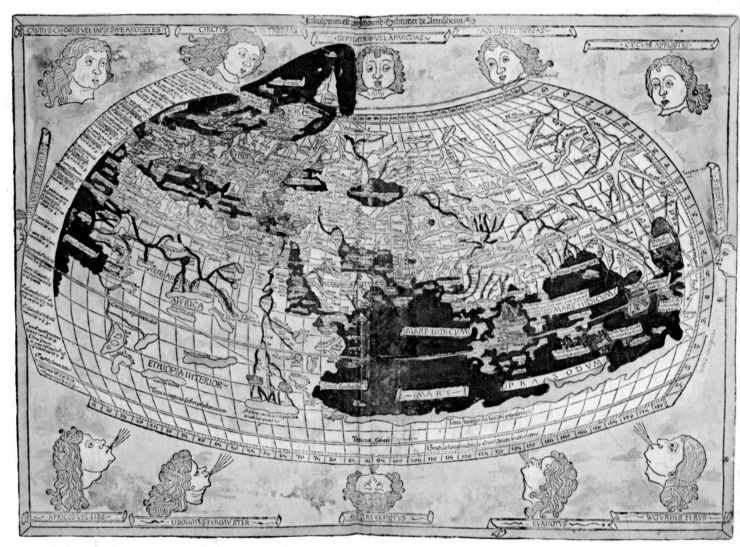

In the three centuries that passed between the time the Portuguese set out on the first cautious exploration of the Atlantic and the last voyage of Captain Cook, Europe discovered the world. In the 15th century Europeans knew only their own continent, part of Asia, and the northern fringes of Africa. More than half the world was a total blank, and much of the rest was known only in dim outline. No European ships had sailed in any of the great oceans except the eastern edges of the Atlantic. The existence of the Pacific, an ocean so large that if all the continents were dropped into it they would sink without trace, was unsuspected.

The discovery of the world was, more exactly, the discovery of the oceans. All the oceans and the seas are connected, so it is possible to sail from any port in the world to any other sea coast. That is what Europeans learned to do. From Columbus to Cook, they sought out all the world's waterways and charted, not always accurately, all the shores that enclosed them. A map of the world after Cook showed the seas and continents much as we know them today, with nearly every island, as well as larger lands, in place. There was only one omission—Antarctica. Its existence was suspected (the icebergs of the south were a likely sign of land somewhere), and in better weather Cook might have sighted it.

Yet in one sense the discovery of the world had only just begun. The position and shape of the islands and continents was known, but not what lay beyond their coasts. The Portuguese sailed around Africa before the end of the 15th century, but at the time of Cook's death Europeans had hardly traveled beyond Africa's coastal plains. No one had penetrated the interior of Australia or New Zealand. Prosperous colonies existed in the Americas, yet the country which was soon to declare its independence as the United States of America was mostly unexplored west of the Mississippi River. Northern and western Canada was unknown territory. Huge areas of South America had never seen a European face, not even the serious, inquiring face of a Jesuit missionary. To explore the newly-discovered lands was the task of the 19th century. Even today there are some places, for example, parts of the Amazon Basin in Brazil, which have never been thoroughly mapped.

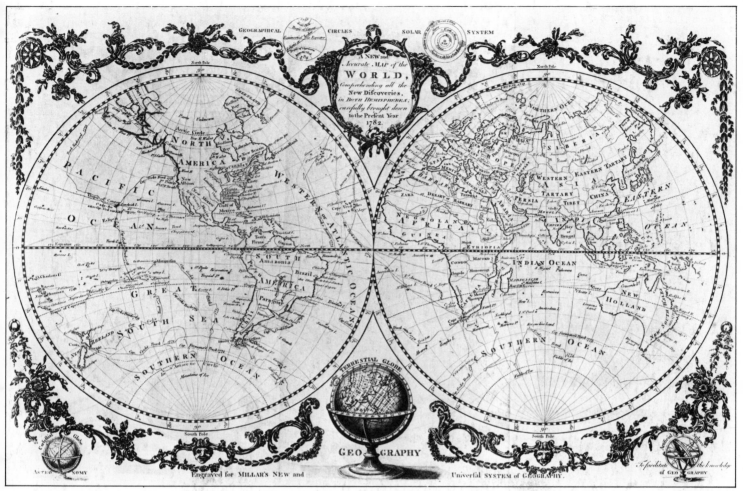

A NEW and Accurate MAP of the WORLD, Comprehending all the New Discoveries, in Both Hemispheres, carefully brought down to the Present Year 1782.

GEO GRAPHY

TERRESTIAL GLOBE

Engraved for MILLAR'S NEW and     Universal SYSTEM of GEOGRAPHY.

**Left: This map shows the world as it was known to educated**

In the 300 years before Cook, the precision of maps, charts, instruments, and methods of navigation had improved enormously. Columbus would have been as bewildered by Cook's instruments as Cook would be by the instruments in an airplane pilot's cockpit. When Columbus was in the West Indies he had believed he was on the other side of the world. Cook's calculation of the position of New Zealand was correct to within a mile or so. On his second voyage Cook carried a chronometer of the type invented a few years earlier by a Yorkshire clockmaker, John Harrison. This was perhaps the single most important advance in navigational methods. The chronometer at last allowed even a navigator less expert than Cook to measure longitude exactly and

**Europeans in 1486 on the eve of the age of discovery. It was based**

without great difficulty. This overcame a problem which had troubled every long-distance voyager since Columbus.

Although the chronometer, and a host of other aids, had made navigation less of a gamble, basic methods had not changed so much. Cook's ship was larger and more reliable, though not much faster, than the caravels of Dias or the ships of Magellan. It was still a wooden vessel, relying wholly on the winds to drive it. The story of the discovery of the world is the story of the triumph of the sailing ship.

Discovery often led to colonization and conquest. It happened with Cortés in Mexico and Pizarro in Peru, and it happened in other countries too. Eventually, most of Africa and much of Asia, as well as North and South

on descriptions of the world by the Greek geographer Ptolemy, who lived in Alexandria in the second century A.D. It is a great improvement on the medieval map on page 6.

**Above: Ptolemy's map was still a far cry from this world map which includes Captain Cook's discoveries. The only major outline that remains to be added is that of Antarctica.**

America, came under the control of Europeans. That was not the purpose of the discoverers, who were usually seeking trade rather than conquest. All the same, the discoveries of Columbus, da Gama and their successors did lead finally to the dominance of Europeans. This had, and still has, a tremendous influence on the way people throughout the world think and feel and live.

# Lifelines

## Vitus Bering
### (1681-1741)

A Danish explorer in Russian service, Bering joined the navy of Peter the Great as a young officer. In 1724, he was selected to lead the expedition to discover whether America and Asia were joined together. When he returned from that expedition, some people thought he had not seen enough to prove whether the continents were joined or not. He then requested permission to make another attempt. His original plans were quite simple, but in the course of discussion they were turned into a much more elaborate expedition— the Great Northern Expedition. During many years of intense hardship, he explored part of the coast of Alaska and the islands of the Aleutian chain. But he was already a dying man. Unfortunately, his ship went aground on Bering Island (named after him) and he died there soon afterwards. The reports of his expedition contained much new material on the geography of the northern Pacific area, but they were not followed up, and his great achievements have never received the credit they deserved.

## Jacques Cartier
### (1491-1557)     ←

Jacques Cartier, a French captain, was born in the Atlantic port of St Malo, Brittany. In 1534 Francis I appointed him to seek a passage to China and find precious metals in the New World. The French king's interest had been sharpened by the recent capture of a Spanish ship loaded with American treasure. Cartier made three expeditions altogether, but the colony he established in Canada did not last long. The stories he told in France of treasures proved to be exaggerated. Though fishermen followed his track to the Newfoundland fisheries, for the time being the French government lost interest in North America.

## Christopher Columbus
### (1451-1506)     ↑

On his first voyage in 1492, this Italian navigator discovered Cuba and Haiti as well as smaller West Indian islands. Columbus then returned in triumph to Spain. He was sent out again the next year with 17 ships to establish colonies in the newly-discovered lands. The expedition was a disappointment. The men left in Haiti the previous year had all died, and Columbus was unable to find Zipangu and Cathay (Japan and China) which he was convinced lay nearby. The first colonial town was built at Santo Domingo. Columbus then discovered Jamaica. On his third voyage (1498) he discovered the

Orinoco River in South America, which he believed flowed from Paradise. At Santo Domingo quarrels broke out and for a time Columbus was thrown in chains by the Spanish governor. He kept the chains, a bitter reminder of his humiliation, for the rest of his life. His fourth and last voyage (1502) was also troubled by quarrels among the Spanish settlers, and by storms. He searched for a strait in Central America, and heard stories of a rich kingdom (probably the Inca empire) which he believed must be China. Columbus returned to Spain disappointed, and still unwilling to believe that he had discovered a continent unconnected with Asia or the Spice Islands.

## James Cook
### (1728-79)

A Yorkshireman of Scots descent, he learned the ways of the sea in Whitby colliers, the same type of ship in which he made his exploring voyages. At the age of 27 he joined the Royal Navy as an able seaman. Intelligent and methodical, he was far above the usual standard of British seaman and soon rose to be master of a ship (below the captain). During the Seven Years' War he took part in the siege of Quebec (1759) and learned how to make charts and surveys. After the war he gained a high reputation for his charts of Newfoundland waters, which he published at his own expense. In spite of the influence of

several high-ranking officers who had gained a good opinion of him as former commanders, he was a surprising choice as captain of the *Endeavour* in 1768 because he was not a 'gentleman'. He only obtained an officer rank in 1768, and did not become a captain until after his second voyage. Cook was not a very colorful character, but was a brilliant navigator whose skill was admired by sailors all over the world. Even the French government, then at war with England, allowed his ship free passage. In spite (or because) of his humble background and lack of education, he showed rare intelligence and compassion in his dealings with rough seamen or Pacific islanders.

power. But the appointment of a new Spanish viceroy of Mexico led to more quarrels and another trip home for some royal support. Even though Cortés had served with the Spanish forces in the siege of Algiers (1541), for which he had to borrow a suit of armor from the Spanish secretary of state, he was coldly received this time by the king. 'Who is this presumptuous man?' the king asked. To which Cortés replied, 'I am the man who has given you more kingdoms than your ancestors left you towns'. He died in Spain, almost forgotten, a few years later.

## John Davis
### (died 1605)

The Englishman John Davis made several voyages in the Atlantic before he began his search for the North-West Passage in 1585. He gave up that attempt after three voyages to north-east Canada, and in 1588 commanded a ship in the defence of England against the Spanish Armada. Three years later he was one of the captains on an expedition that sailed in hope of finding the western outlet of the Passage. The expedition returned unsuccessful, but Davis continued alone to explore the waters of the southern Atlantic, during which he discovered the Falkland Islands. After his return he wrote two very important books about navigation, and he was also the inventor of two navigational instruments, one of them an improvement on the cross-staff. He made several later voyages to the East Indies, and was eventually killed when his ship was attacked by Japanese pirates near Sumatra.

## Martin Frobisher
### (1535-94)

An English captain from Yorkshire, his three voyages to Canada (1576-78) were disappointing, as he had hoped to find the North-West Passage and to find gold and make a fortune. Though a good navigator, he was more of an adventurer and a fighting captain than a true explorer. He was with Sir Francis Drake, his greatest

rival, in an expedition against the Spanish West Indies in 1586. Frobisher was also one of the captains who fought the Spanish Armada (1588), for which he was knighted. In 1594 he led an attack on Brest where he was fatally wounded.

## Vasco da Gama
### (1469-1524)

This Portuguese captain came from an important family and was given the command of the expedition of 1497

## Hernán Cortés
### (1485-1547)

Cortés was an adventurous, hard-drinking Spanish soldier, but also an intelligent and ambitious man. He hoped to create a vast territory for himself in Mexico. As well as conquering the Aztecs, he had to fight jealous Spaniards, and returned to Spain to get the support of the king, Charles V. When he returned to Mexico with his position confirmed, he concentrated on building up his

to India. His father, the first choice for commander, had died, and his brother, the second choice, had refused. In 1502 he made a second voyage to India with 21 well-armed ships. The aim was to establish the Portuguese, by force where necessary, on the coast of East Africa and at Calicut in India. He returned to Portugal in 1503. Twenty years later he was appointed Portuguese viceroy of India, but died soon after arriving there for the third time.

### Henry the Navigator (1394-1460)

Henry the Navigator, a Portuguese prince, fought in the conquest of Ceuta and the Moroccan wars, during which time he gained important information from prisoners about the spice trade routes across the Sahara. He then settled at Sagres, on the most southerly cape of Portugal, where he founded a school of geography and navigation. He welcomed scholars and travelers from many countries, and

encouraged his captains to explore the African coast. The servants of Prince Henry, who traveled to North Africa, Arabia and other parts, provided him with what was probably the best information service in Europe. Travelers who came to tell him of their experiences in some remote country were sometimes surprised to find he knew about them already. The nickname 'the Navigator' was given to Henry by the English long after he had died.

## Ferdinand Magellan
(1480-1521)  ↑

As a young man this Portuguese captain fought for his country in the Far East, taking part in the siege of Malacca (1511) and sailing in search of spice islands. In 1514 he was fighting in Morocco, where he received a wound that left him with a permanent limp. Back in Portugal, Magellan was slighted by the king. He felt his honor had been insulted, and entered the service of Charles V, king of Spain, who gave him command of the voyage to the Pacific via South America (1519). Magellan had probably been thinking over a plan to reach the Spice Islands from the west for many years. In the Philippines he made an alliance with the king of Cebu and was killed by the king's enemies in Mactan.

## Francisco Pizarro
(1475-1541)  ↑

A Spanish adventurer from a poor family, Pizarro was as tough and brutal as Cortés but less intelligent. He sailed to America in 1509. After his remarkable conquest of the Incas,

he organized the running of silver mines in Peru and built a new capital at Lima, on the coast. Pizarro ruled the north of the Inca kingdom and Diego de Almagro, one of his companions on the first expedition from Panama, ruled the south. Each tried to increase his territory at the expense of the other, but in 1538 Pizarro captured Almagro and had him killed. Three years later, a group of Almagro's men murdered Pizarro in the palace he had built for himself.

## Marco Polo  (top)↑
(1254-1324)

Marco Polo, here on his travels, was a boy in Venice when his father and uncle returned from a journey to China. They decided to take him with them on a second expedition. They traveled overland, crossing the high Pamir mountains and the Gobi desert. The Great Khan, Mongol ruler of China, took a fancy to the young Marco and made him his servant. Twenty years passed before

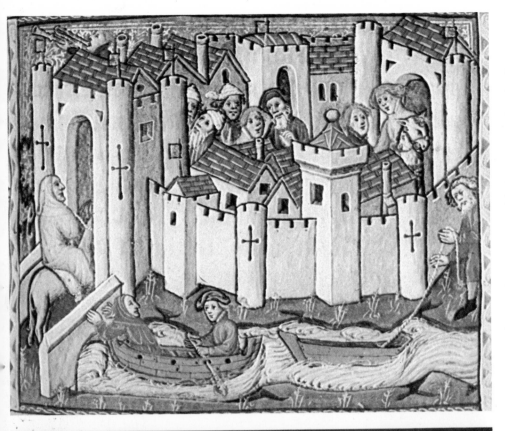

The following year he commanded an expedition against the Spaniards in the Philippines, and retired from the Company's service a few years later.

## St Francis Xavier (1506-1552)

This Jesuit missionary came from a powerful family in Navarre who fell on bad times when the little kingdom was destroyed in the struggle between France and Spain to control it. He studied in Paris, where in 1528 he met Ignatius Loyola, founder of the Jesuits. Xavier was one of the first members of the Order. He was ordained a priest, and planned to go as a missionary to the Holy Land, but there were constant delays. Eventually the Pope sent him instead to the King of Portugal, who wanted missionaries for the Portuguese empire in the East. In India he converted thousands to Christianity—10,000 in one remarkable month in 1544. He complained that his arm was stiff with pouring the water of baptism on all those converts! He spent two years in the Moluccas (the Spice Islands) where he met a native of the newly-discovered country of Japan. From what this man told him, Xavier formed high hopes that the cultured Japanese people would provide a sounder basis for Christianity in the East than the poor fishermen he had labored among in India. In 1549, after long preparations, he reached Japan, the first Christian missionary to visit the country. As he was highly intelligent and tolerant, his mission to Japan went well. But he soon realized that the great civilization of China would provide the key to the Christianization of the East. Despite opposition from the authorities, European as well as Chinese, he eventually set off alone, and arrived on an island off the Chinese coast, near Canton. For three months he tried to gain admittance to China, but he was unable to gain passage to the mainland. Unhappily, he fell ill and died before his last ambition could be fulfilled. Later, his work was carried on by Father Matteo Ricci.

the Polos returned, in 1296, by sea from China through the Indian Ocean to Ormuz, and from there to Constantinople (Istanbul). Marco's book about his travels made him famous. It also encouraged the belief that the Far East could be reached by crossing the Atlantic.

## Abel Janszoon Tasman (1603-59)

The governor of the Dutch East India Company, Van Diemen, sent Tasman in 1642 on a voyage of discovery from Batavia. On this voyage he discovered Tasmania (he named it Van Diemen's Land), and New Zealand, Tonga, and Fiji. The Dutch thought he had not done enough to explore the newly-discovered lands, and sent him out again in 1644. He followed the northern coast of Australia but found none of the rich lands his employers were hoping for; however, he was rewarded and promoted. In 1647 he led a trading voyage to Thailand.

# Datelines

|  | 1300 | 1350 | 1400 | 1450 | 1500 |
|---|---|---|---|---|---|

## EUROPE

Beginning of the Reformation 1517

Small cannon perfected 1320

THE OTTOMAN TURKS

Oil paints invented

**Last Moorish Kingdom in Spain defeated**

Paper manufacture 1270

**HUNDRED YEARS WAR 1337-1453**

**1492**

Cross-staff in common use

**WARS OF THE ROSES 1445-1485**

Magellan sets out around the world 1519

First spectacles made 1285

Movable printing type invented about 1450

THE RENAISSANCE

**Constantinople captured by the Turks 1453**

The Black Death 1348-1350

1494 Treaty of Tordesillas

## AFRICA/ASIA/AUSTRALASIA

SUNG DYNASTY 960-1279

TAMERLANE'S EMPIRE 1369-1405

da Gama reaches India 1498

MING DYNASTY 1368-1644

1260-1269 Niccolo and Matteo Polo to China
1271-1295 Marco Polo to China

Diogo Cão discovers Kongo 1484

St Francis Xavier in Japan 1549

CHINA UNDER THE MONGOLS 1297-1368

Dias sails round Cape of Good Hope 1487

## AMERICAS

INCA EMPIRE 1200-1532

Columbus discovers West Indies 1492

**Cortés captures Tenochtitlán 1521**

Aztecs build capital, Tenochtitlán 1364

First voyage of Cartier 1534

**Pizarro captures Cuzco 1533**

Cabot discovers North America 1497

AZTEC EMPIRE

|  | 1300 | 1350 | 1400 | 1450 | 1500 |
|---|---|---|---|---|---|

## THIRTY YEARS WAR
### 1618-1648

**1701-1713 WAR OF SPANISH SUCCESSION**

Crowns of Spain
and Portugal united
1580

### 1642-1651 ENGLISH CIVIL WAR

**1789 French
Revolution**

Galileo makes a telescope
1609

1668 Isaac Newton makes reflecting telescope

**Defeat of Spanish Armada
1588**

China tea
becomes popular

1775 James Watt perfects
the invention of the
steam engine

Protestantism allowed in Germany
1555

Sextant invented
1731

Barents discovers Spitsbergen
1596

1765 Potato becomes
most popular foodstuff

### 1648-1653 WARS OF THE FRONDE

**Battle of Lepanto
Turks defeated by Christians
1571**

Harrison perfects his chronometer
1761

---

1688 Dampier
in Australia

Cook's first voyage
1768

Jesuit missionaries
in China 1582

**1640 Malacca
conquered by Dutch**

1776 Cook's last voyage

Dutch colony established
at Cape Town
1651

**1736 Tibet becomes part
of Chinese empire**

Tasman sights Tasmania 1642

CH'ING DYNASTY 1644-1912

Christianity suppressed
in Japan 1616

Matteo Ricci in Peking
1601

Calcutta founded by
East India Company
1668

Bering discovers
Bering Strait
1728

---

1576 First voyage of Frobisher

**WAR OF AMERICAN
INDEPENDENCE
1775-1781**

1620 First English colony in New England

Davis discovers
Davis Strait
1585

1616 Schouten and Le Maire round Cape Horn

**1756-1763
SEVEN YEARS WAR**

La Salle sails down
the Mississippi
1681

**1759 Quebec
captured by Britain**

First permanent colony in Virginia
1607

Hudson discovers
Hudson Bay 1610

1626 Dutch colony of New Amsterdam
(New York) founded

French explorers reach Rocky Mountains
1743

# Glossary

**Altitude:** the height of, for example, the sun or a star above the horizon, measured in degrees.

**Azimuth compass:** a bearing compass which seamen use to find the amount of *magnetic variation*.

**Capstan:** revolving 'barrel' for winding cables, and so on. To wind ropes, levers were inserted in holes in the 'barrel'.

**Chronometer:** an accurate, spring-driven timepiece which was suitable for keeping time at sea (pendulum clocks were accurate on land but not at sea).

**Collier:** a ship built specially for the coal trade, with large storage space.

**Jesuits:** a religious order in the Roman Catholic Church founded in the 16th century. Its members became the leading Christian missionaries of the time.

**Latitude and longitude:** the imaginary lines drawn around the earth to locate the position of any place on it. Lines of latitude run east-west, lines of longitude north-south. Lines of latitude are parallel, and measure distance: one degree of latitude equals 60 *nautical miles*. Lines of longitude come together at the poles; they measure time rather than distance: one degree of longitude equals four minutes.

**Lead:** a heavy weight attached to the end of the rope, or lead line, used to plumb the depth of water beneath a ship.

**Lodestone:** a piece of magnetic oxide of iron which indicates magnetic north and can magnetize an iron needle by being stroked against it. Old lodestones, which seemed magical, were often kept in elaborately decorated containers.

**Log line:** a line with knots along it at regular intervals; one end, with a log attached, was thrown overboard, and the ship's speed calculated by the number of knots slipping into the water as the rope was let out.

**Nautical mile:** 1,852 meters, slightly longer than a land mile.

**Reflecting telescope:** containing a curved mirror to expand the image.

**Scurvy:** a disease caused by the lack of vitamin C found in fresh foods; symptoms are terrifying and include loss of teeth and, if the disease is allowed to develop, swollen joints and finally death.

**Sea worms, or teredo worms:** a type of mollusc (the shellfish family) found mostly in warm seas which bore into ships' wooden hulls underwater.

**Spices:** luxury goods, especially pepper, (used to cover up the taste of foul meat), cloves (used to ease toothache), cinnamon and so on; the word was also used to include other luxury goods that would not be classed as spices today, including sugar, silk, even copper.

**Theodolite:** an instrument used in surveying for measuring vertical, horizontal and other angles.

# Index

roverers 14511
il 920 Gra
North Yarmouth Memorial School